Comfort for the Grieving Heart

Comfort for the Grieving Heart

Margolyn Woods

Maureen MacLellan

SunCreek

B O O K S

Allen, Texas

Acknowledgment
The Scripture quotations contained herein are from the *New Revised Standard Version Bible: Catholic Edition* copyright © 1993 and 1989 by the Division of Christian Education for the National Council of the Churches of Christ in the U.S.A. Used by permission. All rights reserved.

Send all inquiries to:
SunCreek Books
An RCL Company
200 East Bethany Drive
Allen, Texas 75002-3804

Telephone: 800-264-0368 / 972-390-6400
Fax: 800-688-8356 / 972-390-6560

Visit us at: **www.thomasmore.com**
Customer Service E-mail: **cservice@rcl-enterprises.com**

Printed in the United States of America

Library of Congress Control Number: 2002102200

5700   ISBN 1-932057-00-5

2 3 4 5 6   07 06 05 04 03

For our children

Sherrilynn, Bryan, Nicolle,
Robyn, Bekki, Kimberly,
Taryn, Matthew, and Adam

Acknowledgments

We want to thank each and every contributor who touched our hearts and shared how God comforted them through difficult circumstances. We truly believe there are crowns waiting in heaven for your willingness to share what God is doing in your lives.

A special thank you to Linda Shepherd and the AWAS Loop, Marita Littauer and the Classervices website, Jan Coleman, Louise Tucker-Jones and Carol McAdoo Rehme for their suggestions, support and help in finding our contributors. Every author should have the privilege—at least once—of working with editors whose excitement and enthusiasm parallel their own! Thank you Debra Hampton and John Sprague of SunCreek Books.

As always, to our families, for your understanding while we become absorbed in each new endeavor, thank you. For your patience during our hours at the computer and while we tie up the phone lines between Oklahoma City and Huntington Beach, our gratitude and love . . . always.

"*L*ike a precious stone with many facets, grief also has a number of dimensions. The stories contained in this book reveal the vast spectrum of feelings associated with grief and allow us to see how God uses this emotion to fashion us into people who reflect His glory."

—LINDA PARMER
NATIONAL SPEAKER COORDINATOR,
STONECROFT MINISTRIES

"*L*ife is filled with difficult circumstances, unwanted loss, and with shattered dreams. *Comfort for the Grieving Heart* reminds all of us that God is at work in these situations even when we can't see the end result. This book will lift your spirits, adjust your perspective, and help you to find hope. Don't miss it!"

—CAROL KENT
PRESIDENT, SPEAK UP SPEAKER SERVICES
AUTHOR, *BECOMING A WOMAN OF INFLUENCE*

"*F*or those who are grieving for whatever reason, these stories will be a blessing. With these personal, touching and sensitive stories, Margolyn and Maureen have brought us into the presence of God's comfort, compassion and love."

—CHARLIE DUKE
APOLLO 16 ASTRONAUT

Contents

Introduction. 11

Collection of Sunsets, Carol Sallee 13

Not Just Any Serviceman, Betty Winslow. 16

Catch of the Day, Maureen MacLellan. 19

Last Breath, Joe Walstad 22

God's Promise, Jack White 24

Staring Death Down, Diana Kruger 27

My Father, Winn Shields 30

God's Whisper, Pat Breckenridge 33

In the Arms of the Shepherd, Judy Gann. 35

The Gift, Valerie Campbell 38

Miracle in Progress, Susan Lugli 40

Perfect in God's Eyes, Denise Springer 43

A Star with My Name on It, Carol Sallee 45

Crossings, Carol McAdoo Rehme. 48

Rebellion and Cancer, Kathy Collard Miller 51

God Revealed, Chuck Dollarhide 55

I Remember Elvis, Anitha Ainsworth 59

From Grief to Gratitude, Karen O'Connor 62

Beloved Parent, Karen Brantley 65

That Special Christmas, Margolyn Woods. 67

Beautiful Feet, Teresa Griggs 71

Never Alone, Cid Davidson 74

A Dollar's Worth of Patriotism, Louise Tucker Jones 77

Time, Joe Walstad 81

Angels on Earth, Lori Pettus 83

Sprinkled with Love, Vickie Jenkins 87

Empty Nest, Full Heart, Maureen MacLellan 90

Journey to Forgiveness, Mike Ozment 92

The Gift of a Song, Rebecca Marshall Farnbach 95

Through God's Eyes, Irene Costilow 100

A Blessing a Day, Gayle Team Smith 103

When Prodigals Don't Return, Louise Tucker Jones 106

Eternal Hope, Bonnie Morgan. 108

My Sister, My Friend, Anonymous 110

A Two-Minute Journey, Pat Drummond 113

Beside Still Waters, Martha Bolton 117

The Miracle of Morgan, Karen Brantley 121

Cindy and Sandy, Cindy Schaus 124

Big Pot of Sauce, Linda Hostelley 127

My Knights in Shining Armor, Linda Dessole Roth 130

Abandoned, But Not by God, Dan Woska 133

A Life Worth Living, Lisa Gilmartin 136

The Blanket, D. Harrison 138

Safely Home, Anonymous 141

Precious Gift, Bonnie Morgan 143

A New Chapter, Jan Coleman 146

Contributors 149

Editors 159

Introduction

$\mathcal{T}$ragedy can tear your world apart. Whether it's the death of a loved one, going through a divorce, a child in trouble or a health crisis . . . grieving hurts. Every situation is different and everyone grieves in their own way.

You may feel anger, guilt, or depression. You may be feeling helpless, insecure or abandoned. The good news is that you are not alone. God loves you and promises to help you through the valleys of life.

Our hope in writing *Comfort for the Grieving Heart* is to encourage you to cling closely to God during difficult times. He promises to never leave you and He will truly lift you above your circumstances.

The Bible tells us, "Come to Me all who are weary and heavy ladened and I will give you rest." Resting in the Lord is the true peace that passes all understanding.

Maureen MacLellan and Margolyn Woods

Collection of Sunsets

I have an odd collection. It's something I can't show to anyone and only God decides when it's time to add to it. I collect sunsets. I started collecting them one summer in Breckenridge, Colorado.

When our family moved from Colorado to Oklahoma, I became incredibly homesick for one particular aspect of Colorado—the Rocky Mountains. To me, they will always be one of the most beautiful parts of God's creation. Two summers after we moved, we went back to Colorado for a vacation. We spent several nights in Breckenridge . . . up in those glorious mountains. I didn't realize until I saw the peaks again, how much I missed them. I also discovered that I had not truly dealt with the grief I felt over our move.

On one night of our vacation, I was overwhelmed by emotion and I told my husband, "I need to take a walk all by myself. I just need some time alone." What I didn't know when I started this walk was that I would come back a different person.

It was near sunset when I started out. As I was walking, I found an amazing place to stop and take a break. Near where I stood, the Breckenridge orchestra was performing in a beautiful, white, translucent tent. I could hear them playing the theme from *Star Wars.* I searched for a place to sit and listen to the incredible music. I found the perfect spot on a "God-made" rock amphitheater beside the river that runs through Breckenridge. The water was rushing because of the snow just beginning to melt off the mountains. I sat there listening to the music God inspires in the hearts of men and the music His rivers make when they are running full.

Have I mentioned the mountains? That night, they were breathtaking. They were still snow-tipped and they surrounded and enveloped me in their magnificence. I watched as He gently guided His orange sun down over tops of His mountains, until it was dark. And then, in my heart, I heard His gentle voice whisper, "Carol, I did this one for you."

That particular sunset is one of my greatest treasures. When I start missing Colorado and the Rocky Mountains I only have to close my eyes, and I am there. I am transported to a place where a river rushes through majestic mountains, accompanied by a full orchestra, with a brilliant sunset as the perfect backdrop. I think God gave this performance to let me know that He understood my sorrow and my longing for this special place in His creation.

It's not the last sunset I've collected. There have been others. Some came at times when I needed a reviving touch deep within my spirit. God spread His pink and orange pallet across the waning blue sky and stirred my soul. Others occurred when I felt afraid or worried and needed to be reminded that God is always in control. Certainly a God who makes each sunset special can handle my life.

Some of the sunsets in my collection exist only as a memory in my heart; others I've captured with a camera. That first sunset in Breckenridge is still the best one—it's the first time I realized that God's hobby was painting them for me.

Carol Sallee

When I look at your heavens, the work of your fingers,
the moon and the stars, that you have established;
what are human beings that you are mindful of them,
mortals that you care for them?
(Psalm 8:3–4)

GOD SPREAD HIS PINK AND ORANGE PALLET ACROSS
THE WANING BLUE SKY AND STIRRED MY SOUL.

Not Just Any Serviceman

A s a lifelong supporter of the military, I was thrilled when my daughter Lisa was appointed to the US Naval Academy's Class of 1994. Remembering the stories, my dad, a World War II navy veteran, used to tell about the importance of mail call, I began a steady stream of letters, cards, and care packages rolling her way.

Then, during December of Lisa's last year at USNA, tragedy struck. Her car of midshipmen, returning from the Army/Navy game, was crushed when a tree came crashing down across the highway. Three girls died. One of them was Lisa.

There would be no more outgoing letters filled with news of home, no more care packages of cookies and candy to be shared with classmates, no more jokes and cartoons to make a frazzled midshipmen and her friends laugh. As a freelance writer, I would continue to write, but my favorite assignment was over. I was no longer "Mailmom."

Then, one evening, I saw a "Dear Abby" column in the newspaper asking people to write to servicemen who were away from their families over the holidays. "If it were my daughter away from home at Christmas and being forgotten at mail call, I'd want someone to write to her," I thought. Since she had planned on becoming a marine, that's who I'd write.

I sat down and wrote a long, newsy letter introducing myself, my hometown, and my family. I mentioned Lisa, her years at USNA, and her tragic death. For a moment, I wondered if mentioning her was wise. I hoped that it wouldn't make the recipients sad, but I knew that I couldn't leave her out. Lisa, after all, was my main reason for writing these letters in the first place.

I addressed several envelopes to "Any Serviceman USMC." I decorated them with rubber stamped bears playing bugles to make them stand out. I stuck a copy of my letter in each one, and dropped them into the mail. I didn't really expect any answers. I knew servicemen were notorious about mail. They always seemed to be able to find time to read mail, but seldom seemed to have time to answer.

Unbeknownst to me, my letters ended up on the USS Guam. Two young marines going through the "Any Serviceman" mail chose letters to fill their lonely hours. One chose a letter whose return address was near his Michigan hometown. The other chose one that was in an envelope decorated with bugle-playing bears.

When they returned to the room they shared, they were surprised to discover they'd chosen letters from the same woman.

Then, as they began to read, they were again surprised, this time to discover that the woman who'd written their randomly chosen letters was the mother of their late classmate, Lisa Winslow.

They immediately wrote back, sharing memories of Lisa and telling me how much it meant to receive news that her family was well. As for me, what a blessing, so close to the anniversary of my daughter's death to be assured that Lisa had not been forgotten!

Several years later, another classmate of Lisa's wrote that he too, had received an "Any Serviceman" letter from me that Christmas. He found such comfort in both my letter and the coincidence that had put it in his hands. My envelopes may have been addressed to "Any Serviceman," but God knew their names—and mine.

⟜ *Betty Winslow*

For the eyes of the Lord range throughout the entire earth,
to strengthen those whose heart is true to Him.
(2 Chronicles 16:9)

NO LONGER IN MY ARMS; ALWAYS AND FOREVER IN MY HEART.

Catch of the Day

Dad sat up in his hospital bed, "Where are my boots?"

He was insistent upon getting up, dressed, and out of there.

Calmly, I tried to get him to stay in bed, "Dad, you need to rest now."

"Can't" he replied, "Got to get out to the lake."

"Whatever for, Dad?"

"Your mom said she wanted the catch of the day for dinner, so I'd better get to it."

I'd found it was best to go along with dad when he got like this, so I told him we would go out to the lake in a little while, after he rested. He lay back against his pillow.

I looked over at mom. The tears were welling up in her eyes. This was not the husband of fifty years she had known. This was not the corporate executive, her protector, her confidant. This was a man in the later stages of Alzheimer's disease, disoriented and confused. His beloved lake was 3,000 miles away and he didn't have any boots.

I walked over to comfort mom, to put my arm around her. But as soon as I did, dad was getting out of bed again.

"No, Dad, the doctor wants you to stay in bed." I rushed back to him to help him lay back down again, no time for mom right now. "You need to rest. The nurse will be bringing your dinner in a few minutes. The hospital menu says you'll be having the catch of the day."

"Yup, I'll get out to the lake and catch it." Here we go again.

"No, Dad, the nurse will bring it, and while you eat, I'm going to take mom out for dinner, then we will be right back."

"Oh! Okay, honey." Did he get it?

"Where'd you put my fishing pole?" Nope.

I rang for the nurse. Maybe she could distract him while I took mom out to eat. She came in and started to prepare him for his dinner. He settled back and seemed very calm. She chitchatted with him while mom and I prepared to sneak out. Then she said the dreaded word, "You'll be having the catch of the day tonight."

Dad's feet were once again heading for the floor. The absurdity of this situation was beginning to resemble something out of a *Three Stooges* movie. Concerned, I glanced back at mom. The second our eyes met she burst out in laughter. I started to laugh too. The laughter was contagious. Dad started laughing and then so did the nurse. While laughing, dad seemed to forget all about fishing so mom and I hugged him and left him with his nurse. We giggled about the catch of the day in the elevator and all the way to the car. This was the first time mom had laughed about the disease. Laughter was the best medicine. From this point on mom and I were better able to deal with the disappoint-ment and frustration of dad's disease. A little humor helped a lot along the way. For dinner that night mom and I had Mexican food. We don't care much for fish.

Maureen MacLellan

A cheerful heart is good medicine,
but a downcast spirit dries up the bones.
(Proverbs 17:22)

SOME PURSUE HAPPINESS—OTHERS CREATE IT.

Last Breath

ith big black eyes
and a small wet nose,
You were the bundle of fur
that I chose.

Small and frail, you peered up at me,
"Take me home" was your plea.

Snug in my arms our friendship did start,
From the first wet lick you owned my heart.

Walks in the park and romps in the grass,
Rides in the car as you fogged up the glass.

Quiet still nights as the cold wind blew,
The years did pass as the friendship grew.

The time has come when we must part,
I dreaded this day from the very start.

The days grew to months and then to years,
As you take your last breaths you lick my tears.

Concerned about me to the dying end,
My heart is breaking as you leave my friend.

I know it was His plan from the moment we met,
God did bless me with you for a pet.

The love that you gave was from God above,
Only He could spare this much love.

Your life was devoted to loving me,
So, now is the time I must set you free.

Free from the pain that old age brings,
Into the heaven where angels sing.

There is no doubt in my mind you see,
When I get to heaven you'll be waiting for me.

Joe Walstad

He heals the brokenhearted and binds up their wounds.
(Psalm 147:3)

ANIMALS ARE OFTEN A PICTURE OF GOD'S LOVE.

God's Promise

September 11, 2001, more than any other single event in history, has changed our world forever. Personally, my first fear was not safety, but how 9-11 would affect the careers and lifestyles of my wife and myself as successful artists.

Yes, greed was the first thing that raced through my mind. I was immediately self-centered, remembering my mate's past struggles and her restored self-esteem; how hard we had worked to this point in life to achieve our goals. As the news unfolded my fear changed to anger. Then about noon on that day, reality took over. I began to think of others.

I remembered a little saying about real joy, JOY = Jesus, Others, Yourself.

My mate Mikki and I stopped and asked our Lord Christ Jesus to rid our hearts of fear and redirect our thoughts to others. Others, for us, were our dear friends Diane and Earl Davis. Diane is a flight attendant with American Airlines. She was based in Washington, D.C., and had recently moved to Miami, Florida. We knew, but for the Grace of God, she could have been on one of those four crashed flights. How was she doing? What could we do to help her? Since she was the only person we knew on a personal level who had connections with this catastrophic event, we let her become our main focus. Diane knew several of the murdered victims. She heard accounts of friends being tied up and having their throats slashed while others watched. She also faced the possibility that her next flight could be her last one.

"How are you dealing with all of this?" we asked.

"My moods are like a roller coaster, from crying to mad!" she answered, "but I am doing okay. Some of my friends are taking it a lot harder. They do not know Jesus Christ. I believe with all my heart it is Jesus who is getting me through this trial."

She went on, "On the first of September, I was having my quiet time. God gave me a verse and told me to meditate on it for the month. I had been given scriptures for a day and even for a week, but as I told Earl, I had never been told to meditate on a scripture for an entire month. I didn't think much about it until I arrived home September 13 and was alone again with God. I now knew why I had been given this particular scripture; it was to shine the light on God's promise.

Jack White

25

. . . those who listen to me will be secure
and will live at ease, without dread of disaster.
(Proverbs 1:33)

JOY = JESUS, OTHERS, YOURSELF.

Staring Death Down

he lump in my breast was the size of a walnut by the time I noticed it. I knew better than to delay and immediately made an appointment. The doctor referred me to a specialist. "If he can't see you within a week or so, call me," he cautioned. "You shouldn't wait longer than that."

My emotions churned. This was just like eleven years earlier. When our pediatrician saw the size and hardness of our eight-month-old's abdomen, he said, "I don't know what it is, but check your son into Children's Hospital first thing Monday." By the next week's end, we learned that Mallon had inoperable liver cancer. During three months of treatments, I prayed fervently for his healing. Several friends encouraged us in those beliefs, and

I became convinced that God would heal our baby. Then, on the night of Mallon's first birthday, his weakened heart stopped. I was convinced that God had failed me, yet turning away was unthinkable. "Be gentle with me," I begged Him. "I'm clinging to the end of my rope."

Then I sensed being cradled in God's arms. Every time I prayed about my mundane concerns, God answered. Was my sheltered time over? Must I trust God again with cancer? Since God had not healed Mallon, how could I believe He would heal me? The days dragged by until my appointment. Meanwhile, I tackled painting the house trim. "Lord," I prayed at the top of the ladder, "please help me trust You." A flock of birds flew overhead, and I remembered Jesus' words, "Are not two sparrows sold for a penny? Yet not one of them will fall to the ground apart from the will of your Father. . . . So don't be afraid; you are worth more than many sparrows" (Matthew 10:29–31).

I did not always understand God's workings, but I knew He could dissolve the lump if He chose. I reached across my chest toward the eaves, and the lump rippled against my upper arm. It was as large and firm as ever—or had it grown? Tormenting doubts returned.

At the specialist's office, surgery had delayed the doctor. "Oh, Lord, help me not to worry." A gentle peace descended. "I have plans for you," I sensed God saying. An hour and forty minutes later, the doctor arrived. "I'm not sure what the lump is," he admitted. "If it's a cyst, we can aspirate the fluid. Let's try that first." Soon he was holding a vial of amber liquid. "It looks good," he announced. Lab tests later confirmed his optimism. Relief flooded me. The lump had been harmless—but more important, God had spared me. Most of all, I really had heard God's comforting words. "I have plans for you," He assures us. As the specifics of those plans unfold in our lives, we can be certain they'll be in our best interests.

Diana Kruger

"Thereby command you: Be strong and courageous;
do not be frightened or dismayed,
for the Lord your God is with you wherever you go."
(Joshua 1:9)

NOTHING LIES OUTSIDE THE REACH OF PRAYER
EXCEPT THAT WHICH IS OUTSIDE THE WILL OF GOD.

My Father

My father always loomed over me. He always seemed to know the right thing to say and do. I, on the other hand, said and did everything wrong. He must have had his faults but to a boy of six, he never made a mistake—never.

Like everyone in our neighborhood, our parents didn't have much money, yet they managed to give us twenty-five cents every Saturday as an allowance. It seemed like a lot of money to us, and in those days it was enough to make us sick on candy and soda. This particular Saturday, my friend Quint and I spent all of our money early in the morning. When we passed Our Lady of Fatima Church, Quint said we should go in and pray. He was seven and had received First Communion so I was sure he must know as much about the church as anyone. Once we were at the altar praying, I didn't want to stop before Quint. He prayed for, what seemed to a six-year-old, a long time. I had already said all the prayers I knew, so I began to look around. I always liked being in church. I was too young to understand about the tabernacle and what it represented but I felt it all the same.

I could smell the candles and lingering incense. I looked at the different colors—the brown statues—red glass candleholders and the way the light danced at the feet of the saints. Then, my eye caught the color of green. Not the votive candles but something just inside the altar rail. It was a dollar bill.

I whispered the news to Quint. Quint suggested I should get it, he said he couldn't—something about accountability. Taking the dollar didn't take much effort and we were off to the store. Somehow having a dollar to share (two weeks' extra allowance) didn't seem to be the blessing we thought. We were too full to buy more sweets, so we wasted the money on cheap toys. It's just as well they were so easily broken as we would never have dared take them home.

By the end of the day, I had learned a lesson. Having extra money didn't give me any particular joy. I only spent it on stuff I didn't want and couldn't keep.

I was feeling kind of bad. When I saw Quint again, it was late in the afternoon. He said he felt the same and had gone to confession to tell the priest. It never occurred to me the priest would not know of my involvement. I didn't know about the seal of the confessional. I was sure the priest had called my father and told him what we had done.

As night began to fall, I wandered through the streets, afraid to go home. There was little doubt in my mind what would happen when I did. The cold haziness of the sky made me feel lonely and hungry. My whole body ached from walking. I wished I could go home.

Finally, I couldn't stand it any longer. As I walked in the door, my father looked at me silently. He knew I wouldn't have stayed out so late unless there was something wrong. He asked what I had done. I thought he knew, so I told him the whole story.

After I finished, I stood sobbing. My father reached out and drew me to his side. He told me I would have to go with him to talk to the priest. We would see what he wanted me to do about paying back the money. Then he hugged me. I didn't feel lonely, hungry, or tired anymore.

My father always loomed over me. He always seemed to know the right thing to say and do. I, on the other hand, said and did everything wrong. He must have had his faults, but to a boy of six, he never made a mistake—never.

Win Shields

I have no greater joy than this, to hear that my children are walking in the truth.
(3 John 2:4)

TEACHING CHILDREN TO COUNT IS NOT AS IMPORTANT
AS TEACHING THEM WHAT COUNTS.

God's Whisper

At 12:40 A.M., two men came to my door. They told me the plane had run into trouble immediately after departure. The wings had iced and the gyroscope had failed. The pilot declared an emergency, but as he tried to land, the single engine plane had stalled, crashed, and exploded.

Nothing in life can prepare you for the pain of losing a child. Even the idea of it was so painful that my mind would run away from it. Yet I had to deal with it. My only son, Jason, was gone from this earth. I would never hear his laughter, feel his hugs, or see him grow into an adult. I had read that if our loved ones are with the Lord and He is within us, then they can't be far away. This took on real meaning for me. Truly, I did feel Jason was very close. Although I could not see or touch him, he seemed just beyond my fingertips. Heaven seemed very near.

I had heard others say that Heaven becomes much sweeter and more real when a loved one dies. That proved true for me. My feet seemed much less rooted to this earth. Words are so inadequate to describe the way God ministered to me. He used people to show me His love through their touch and kind eyes. He used their arms to enfold me, their hands to soothe me. Their many cards and letters assured me that He cared. It somehow gave me permission to rest in God's big hands until I was able to stand again.

I still miss Jason, and my grief overwhelms me at times. When allowing myself to think about those last few moments before the plane crashed, I feel weak. At these times I call out to God, and He always whispers, "Jason is fine. I've got him. He's home." There is a peace that truly passes all understanding. I know that Jason is home . . . and one day, I will be there, too.

Pat Breckenridge

"*I will never leave you or forsake you.*"
(Hebrews 13:5b)

SORROW LOOKS BACK, WORRY LOOKS AROUND, AND FAITH LOOKS UP.

In the Arms of the Shepherd

With downcast eyes and sagging shoulders, I crept across the parking lot of the medical center. The cumulative effect of weeks of radiation treatments for breast cancer had taken their toll on my already weakened body. I crawled into my car and drove home.

As I entered my bedroom, I noticed the flashing message light on the answering machine. When I touched the "play" button my dad's tense voice filled the room. My mother was in a coma.

"No!" I cried aloud. "That can't be! She sounded so strong when I talked to her last night!"

With trembling fingers I hit the "playback" button. The message was the same. I was to come as soon as possible.

Friends helped me pack. Within two hours I boarded a plane to San Diego. I prayed throughout the seemingly endless flight—for my mom and for me. "Lord, give me the strength and grace to face whatever is awaiting me when I step off this plane." My heart pounded as I limped into the terminal. Scanning the crowd, my eyes rested on my sister. One glance at Peggy's face told me I was too late. Mom had died. Someone screamed. It was me.

Numb with grief and battling constant fatigue, I moved through the next oppressive hours and days sustained by God alone. The Lord carried me through the interminable details of planning my mother's memorial service. With God's comfort, I comforted members of my family.

My body shook as I stood before two hundred fifty people at my mother's memorial service. Grief, nervousness, and the side effects of radiation treatments almost silenced me. However, bolstered by God's enabling strength, I spoke of my mother's tremendous influence on my life.

My radiation regime forced me to return to Tacoma immediately. I dreaded leaving my family. Who would share memories of my mom and the pain of her death with me?

My dad and I sat in the airport boarding area. Dreading the moment we would say good-bye, we barely spoke. As I stood to board the plane, Dan and Yvonne Larson walked up to the check-in counter. Dan was one of the pallbearers at my mother's memorial service. Not only were the Larsons on my flight, they were seated in the row in front of me. Instead of a sad and lonely flight home, God provided the opportunity to share treasured memories with friends who had known my mom since high school. The next few months were filled with anguish as I battled the side effects of radiation and grieved the loss of my mother.

Yet God sustained me during those agonizing months. When grief and weakness threatened to overwhelm me, the Lord carried me "close to His heart." In His arms I found the strength to travel through a dark and lonely valley.

Judy Gann

He will feed his flock like a shepherd;
he will gather the lambs in his arms,
and carry them in his bosom,
and gently lead the mother sheep.
(Isaiah 40:11)

COINCIDENCE IS WHEN GOD CHOOSES TO REMAIN ANONYMOUS.

The Gift

*L*ast month I felt like the rug had been jerked out from under me. My husband called from work and said he was coming home. The company was downsizing and he had been let go after eighteen years of service. My immediate reaction was fear. What did the future hold? I was scared and in a state of shock for several days. All I could do was cry.

Then my husband asked, "How would you feel if I gave you a huge gift with a gorgeous big bow on top?"

"I would be excited and anxious to open it," I answered.

He then asked, "Would you be afraid of it?"

"No," I responded.

"Exactly!" he said. "I wouldn't give you anything to harm you because I love you! Our Heavenly Father loves us even more than I love you. He wants to bless us and not harm us. He has promised to meet our needs and as our needs are being met we can know that we are blessed."

Even though the situation was not good I began to feel God's peace, comfort, and guidance. I knew God had us in the palm of His hand. We were protected and in His care. We believe that He is taking us to a better place. Even though we still don't know exactly where that is, we are excited and looking forward to seeing His plan unfold. As each day goes by, I feel like God is restoring my hope and joy.

Before this all happened I had a false sense of security. I put my security in the company and in the paycheck that my husband was bringing home. God is now showing us that He is in control of the situation. We still don't know the final outcome, but we do know that God is good. It has been a step-by-step process, but we are learning a lot and growing in the Lord every day. I can say that now my security and trust are in Him. According to His Word, our future is in His hands and His plan is to prosper us and not to harm us. He gives us hope and a future.

Valerie Campbell

. . . *But those who wait for the Lord shall renew their strength, they shall mount up with wings like eagles, they shall run and not be weary, they shall walk and not faint.*
(Isaiah 40:31)

THE SHORTEST DISTANCE BETWEEN A PROBLEM AND THE SOLUTION
IS THE DISTANCE BETWEEN YOUR KNEES AND THE FLOOR.

Miracle in Progress

Eight years ago I was lying in a hospital bed looking out the window, watching the world go on around me. Everyone and every-thing seemed to be moving, except me. I was trapped inside a severely burned body and my backbone had been shattered. The pain was like no other in this world. I now understood the term "wracked with pain" as my body shook uncontrollably. I could hear myself screaming inside to be released from this horror I was experiencing. Tears poured from my eyes continually but my burned arms and hands could not reach to wipe them away. I was imprisoned in a world of the unknown.

As I watched the seasons change, I realized my life would never be the same again. I was facing the biggest challenge of my forty-seven years and I was falling into the deepest pits of despair and depression. Georgia Shaffer, in her book *A Gift of Mourning Glories,* describes the darkest time in my life when she writes, "Winter existed both on the inside and outside of me." For me there seemed to be no sunshine, and it would be that way for a very long time.

My entire life had been full of challenges and I knew my faith in Jesus had always upheld me in the past. This time I would have to trust and allow Him to carry me through this healing and restoring season. I had my son bring in a CD player and my praise and worship music, and also the Bible on tape. The music played all through the day and filled my soul with encouragement. At night the Bible indwelled me as I tried to sleep, and it gave me hope.

Each day was full of extreme pain as I experienced two-hour bandage changes each morning and each night. I would ask my nurses to pray with me each time before they began. I knew the routine by heart, and every time I saw nurses, doctors, or therapists come in my room, I would know they were there to hurt me. My depression was deep and my anxiety was high. I always knew Jesus was there with me; He did not make the pain go away, but He made it bearable. The Lord worked through many family members and friends to help meet the needs I had. The cards and posters hung all around my bed, reminding me how much I was loved. A sign stating "Miracles in Progress" was placed on a wall over the head of my bed.

A miracle is definitely what our family needed. My husband and daughter were in the motor-home accident with me. This was the most difficult season of our lives, a reminder of how fast life can change. Everyone will have storm clouds gather at some time in their life. I hope you will find comfort in knowing the Lord carried us through our horrible time, giving us hope and showing once again His faithfulness and love.

Today life is good and our family lives together on a beautiful ranch. Our physical bodies are scarred but our hearts are pure, refined by fire. I now work with burn survivors and their families. The struggles and trials have been many. I now see them as opportunities to show God's love, perseverance, patience, and never-ending love.

Susan Lugli

Therefore, let those suffering
in accordance with God's will entrust themselves
to a faithful Creator, while continuing to do good.
(1 Peter 4:19)

WHAT HAPPENS TO MEN AND WOMEN IS LESS SIGNIFICANT
THAN WHAT HAPPENS WITHIN THEM.

Perfect in God's Eyes

"Denise, Drew is really, really sick. He needs an operation and may not make it." Those are the first words I heard when I awoke from an emergency C-section. My husband and my obstetrician were preparing me to see what they were seeing. God had a better plan.

I opened my groggy eyes to a perfect little leg. I saw nothing more. Not the incubator that held our son. Not the respirator that breathed for him. I just saw a plump, healthy leg.

Our baby had a diaphragmatic hernia that allowed his abdominal organs to slide into his chest. The pressure caused one lung to collapse and kept the other from forming fully. He couldn't breathe and, according to doctors, would likely die even with his impending surgery.

Before this moment, the thought of having a sick baby had hardly entered my mind. I was meticulously careful during my pregnancy, so I thought everything would be fine. Now I ached for that fantasy, but it wasn't meant to be.

Drew had a strong will to live but grief and exhaustion made it incredibly hard for me to function. I knew I couldn't wallow in debilitating grief while my baby fought for his life. He needed me to be his cheerleader.

When my strength wavered I would remember the picture of Drew's healthy little leg and know it was a gift from God. I felt He was saying, "In the end you'll have a healthy little son to match the picture I showed you."

Today Drew is seventeen years old and, aside from scars and hearing aids, you'd never guess he wasn't physically perfect. The road was long and hard, and I wouldn't wish it on anyone. However, God brought me closer to Him through the traumatic months of Drew's illness. That part of the experience I wouldn't trade for anything.

⎯⎯⎯⎯⊃ *Denise Springer*

*L*et us hold fast to the confession of our hope without wavering, for he who promised is faithful. (Hebrews 10:23)

I AVOID LOOKING FORWARD OR BACKWARD,

AND TRY TO KEEP LOOKING UPWARD. (Charlotte Bronte)

A Star with My Name

I had suffered from depression off and on throughout my entire adult life, but it was especially bad after the birth of my third child. I never really had a good reason to be depressed. I had a wonderful Savior, a great marriage, three happy kids, good health, a beautiful home, a supportive church—all the pieces were there for happiness. But I wasn't happy.

Some days, it was like a dark cloud came from nowhere and settled heavily on my brain. It was difficult to make the simplest decisions. A sink full of dirty dishes felt like the most over-whelming job I'd ever been given. The sadness overshadowed everything and pulled me down until I thought I'd never feel happy again. On those days, I sat on the couch, trying to make myself as "small" as I could, moving as little as possible. If I didn't move, then I didn't have to think. If I didn't think, then I didn't have to feel.

It was during one of those "dark periods" that our family drove from Colorado to Oklahoma for a brief summer visit to see our parents. We decided to drive at night so it would be cooler. My husband, who did the late-night driving, usually listened to music on his Walkman while the kids and I slept.

But this particular night, I wasn't sleeping. Instead, I was contemplating taking my own life. I had entertained this thought before, but never so seriously. I was tired of the work of living and the overwhelming, day-to-day battle of being a wife, a mother, and a pastor's family. It seemed in my mind that the best choice was to just be done with life.

I began to think about jumping out of the car, onto that dark Kansas highway. I felt so crazy, to be thinking about killing myself—especially in this particular manner—while my children slept in the backseat and my husband drove. Funny thoughts even played through my mind: "Won't that really hurt?" "How many miles before they notice I'm gone?"

Before I went any further, I decided to pray one more time: "God, I know all the promises about how You created me with a special purpose. I know all the verses about a special plan for my life. But I am tired. Life just seems so hard. You know what I am thinking about doing. If You have any reason for me to stay in this car, You need to show me pretty quick."

This prayer was barely out of my lips when the brightest shooting star blazed across that dark Kansas sky. No one else in the car saw the star—it belonged to me. Its brilliance saved my life. God showed me through a perfectly timed flash of light that He loved me and that my life was worth the effort He had taken to create it. I took my hand off the handle of the car door, knowing that God had something special planned for me.

These days when I see a shooting star, I am reminded of the night that God was powerful enough to give my life back to me. I would like to say that it's been "smooth sailing" since—I know better. I do know it will never be hopeless again, and somewhere in a galaxy far, far away, I have a shooting star with my name on it to prove it!

Carol Sallee

Lift up your eyes on high and see: Who created these? He who brings out their host and numbers them, calling them all by name.
(Isaiah 40:26)

GOD LIFTS ME UP WHERE I BELONG.

Crossings

*S*he was death's handmaiden.

And Sue took the job gladly. The hushed night hours lent a kinship to her caregiving. A dim lamp haloed the bed with its circle of light, almost pulsing with the patient's measured breaths. Some saw this as a deathwatch. Sue saw it as a ritual journey—as natural as all the deliveries she once assisted—and she was merely there to attend to the boarding pass. To her, it was simply a trip with God as the destination.

The thick soles of her worn, comfortable shoes padded across the room. Sue smoothed the bleached bedsheet, tucked in the thin blanket, and gently straightened the man's head to a more comfortable position. She plucked spent blossoms from a vase of daisies, tidied the hospital stand, and scooted a vinyl chair closer to the bed. The oak frame groaned as she sank her ample weight into it.

The end wasn't always peaceful. Sometimes it arrived with distress, pain, and fear but, more often, the opposite was true. Either way, families wanted someone in attendance and, for one reason or another, many couldn't be there themselves. For some it was simply too painful; others couldn't spare the time; a few families lived too far away.

That's why Sue had replaced her cozy retirement slippers with her old nursing shoes. To tend the dying for the living. She felt comfortable volunteering to sit with terminally ill patients between the deep, holy hours of midnight and morning. At seventy-eight years of age, she acknowledged that arthritis had crept in, robbing her of sleep, anyway. And it felt good to be useful again— especially with a patient like this one.

She and Arnold Taylor went way back. Why, they had attended the same schools, the same church, the same potluck dinners, and the same weddings and funerals in this small Iowa town. So it was only fitting that she attend his death, and Sue knew it wouldn't be long. She recognized the signs: his skin was mottled, his hands and feet discolored. And, since tonight's shift began, she'd already seen a change in his breathing.

The patient stirred slightly and moaned.

"It's okay, Arnie." Sue's strong, corded hand blanketed his, gently stroking the parchment skin.

His eyes, as pale as a denim work shirt that had suffered too many washings, opened and stared beyond her.

"You've had a good life, Arnie, but there's an even better one waiting." She reached over to caress his grizzled cheek. "When you're ready, Arnie, just cross over because God is waiting. It's okay. When you're ready."

And then it happened.

She felt it at almost the same time as she witnessed it: his wide-eyed look of radiant joy and then his hands reaching toward a presence. Sue glanced hopefully at the foot of the bed, all the while knowing she wouldn't see anyone there. She never could.

Then it came, an almost tangible release—as soft as the tiny last sigh that puffed from Arnie's smiling lips while his arms sank back to the bed. Expelling her own pent-up breath, Sue's trembling fingers brushed his eyelids closed.

Glancing at the clock, she noted the time, then paused to feel once more the solemn sacredness in the moment. Fleeting yet perceptible. Hopeful—and hallowed. She felt privileged to behold it.

With a farewell glance toward the bed and a silent prayer of gratitude for a life well-lived, Sue walked toward the door. Now it was time to tend the living. She pulled a list from her pocket with the names and telephone numbers of an entire family. Arnie's family. She had relatives to notify, a wife to comfort, children to console.

She was life's handmaiden.

⌐➲ *Carol McAdoo Rehme*

As I was with Moses, so I will be with you;
I will not fail you or forsake you. (Joshua 1:5b)

THERE IS PLENTY OF HEAVENLY MUSIC FOR THOSE WHO ARE TUNED IN.

Rebellion and Cancer

My fifteen-and-a-half-year-old daughter, Darcy, was going through a rebellious time. She had always been strong-willed and her teenage years were the epitome of her wanting-to-be-in-control viewpoint of life. She had begun talking on the phone with a seventeen-year-old friend about his problems with a girlfriend. Before we knew it, Darcy had become the new girlfriend, even though she wasn't supposed to date until she turned sixteen.

Whenever my husband, Larry, and I reminded her of our rule, she turned surly and argumentative. I was stunned by her behavior. Why is she so angry at us? What is going on in the relationship between this boy and Darcy? Is she staying true to the purity we taught her? Time and again we tried to reach out to her.

I felt worried and helpless; nothing seemed to make any difference. Each time we tried to talk to her, she closed off emotionally and wouldn't respond.

Unfortunately, this wasn't the only worry we were facing. A mole on Larry's chest had been growing and changing color. The test results confirmed it was melanoma. Within a few days, more tissue would have to be removed to determine if the cancer had gone inside his body. *Is Larry's life in danger? Will I become a widow at such an early age?* I wondered. I prayed over and over again, "Lord God, I don't want to lose my best friend." We were shaken; worry tried to turn my wondering into fear.

After the additional tissue was removed and sent for testing, we again waited for the test results. As we did, Darcy's rebellious attitude continued to create additional tension in our family. One evening, Larry and I decided we had to try again to reach out to her.

"Darcy, honey, we love you," Larry began. "We want to know what's going on so that we can work through our differences." Darcy sat immobilized, her face just as impassive as ever. I spoke up, "Darcy, we really do want to talk this out. We love and care about you." Darcy still sat silent, her lips pursed in defiance. Larry and I looked at each other, feeling hopeless and helpless. "Oh, God," I prayed silently. "Please help us. What will get through to her?"

Then without any explanation, her face softened, her arms came down and she began talking to us. We were thrilled! For forty-five minutes we talked and talked. We found out she wanted to keep a pure relationship with her boyfriend and that her values were similar to ours. As we all talked, Larry and I shot glances at each other with a look that questioned, "Why is she finally talking with us?" We had no idea.

When we were finished, Darcy stood up and walked over to the bedroom door. She put her hand on the knob, opened it slightly and then hesitated. She looked back at us with a confused look and said, "I don't know why I'm talking to you like this." Then as if the reason had occurred to her, she continued, "I guess it's because Daddy has cancer."

God had used for good what we thought could never be used for good: cancer. As a strong-willed teenager, the Lord knew that only something as severe as possibly losing her daddy to cancer would make her see life with a different perspective. Darcy never returned to that state of rebellion and today we all have a fantastic relationship. She is a college graduate, a delightful young woman who loves God, and the coauthor with me of the book *Staying Friends With Your Kids* (Harold Shaw Publishers). We rejoice that Larry has been free of melanoma for over ten years.

As God has so faithfully shown us many times before, all things work together for good for those who love God. Since then, I've claimed that promise over and over again as a solution to worry. Even if what I worry about comes true, God promises to use it for good. Therefore I don't have to worry because it's really all in God's plan.

Kathy Collard Miller

We know that all things work together for good for those who love God, who are called according to his purpose.
(Romans 8:28)

DO YOUR BEST; LET GOD DO THE REST.

God Revealed

Our three children, Chuck, Ajen, and Ashley, were just entering their college years. My wife, Pat, and I suddenly realized just how much of our lives had been invested in our children and their activities for the past eighteen years. It had been a time of so many joys. Yet now we began to question our own relationship. Had we stopped being a real couple sometime during those child-raising years? The transition led to a crisis for us, one in which we needed God's strength and healing like never before.

The seeds of my own personal crisis were sown as I grew up the oldest child of an alcoholic parent. I developed a need to always be in charge of things, to be in control, and to have the appearance of not having any problems. As an adult, I strove to accomplish things and be successful, at least in worldly terms. I worked diligently to be a good provider for my family, a good boss at work, and a good leader in numerous community and church leadership positions.

I didn't realize it, but all those responsibilities were much too heavy, much more than one person should take on. From the outside, I'm sure people thought I had it all together. However, on the inside, I slipped into a valley of depression. From my point of view, life's opportunities began to look like obstacles. I faced mountains of fear and roaring anxiety every day. I struck out verbally at people, especially at Pat and others to whom I was closest, hoping people would go away and leave me alone. I found it more and more difficult to make decisions. I doubted my desire or my capability to accomplish anything in my work as a lawyer. Like an injured animal, I was irritable, easily provoked, and usually looking for a way to hole up by myself in my den. Instead of sharing my fears and problems with my life mate, I tried to hide them so Pat would think I still had everything under control. I built walls to prevent others from seeing what I judged to be my weaknesses. I found myself locked behind those walls to the point that even though I was a Christian, I could hardly see God. Our marriage was headed in a direction which I would have considered unthinkable only a few years earlier.

Finally, I got to a point where I couldn't take it anymore. I prayed that God would show me a way out. Through friends, God led Pat and me to a marriage encounter weekend. God spoke to my heart in ways that broke down the walls that I had let build up all those years. I was finally able to reveal my fears and anxieties to Pat. I was afraid she would reject me. Instead she opened up to me and listened to me with her whole heart. Pat accepted me just the way I was. Through that special time, I finally realized that Pat loved me unconditionally, and that God loved me unconditionally, too. I began to learn how to listen to Pat's feelings as well. We began to sense God healing our marriage. I felt so happy and free that I wanted to dance and sing!

God also led me to a Christian counselor. Working with my counselor opened up new insights for me. For years I was embarrassed to admit that I couldn't solve all my problems myself. So I had resisted asking anyone for help. Now God spoke to me through that wonderful counselor as well. I was amazed as my faith deepened, and old wounds were exposed to light and healed.

These events occurred some thirteen years ago. My life has been totally renewed since those days. I have a wonderful marriage. I trust God much more readily. I enjoy life, am open to learning new things, and I love people. I truly believe the words of the prophet: "Every valley shall be raised up, every mountain and hill made low; the rough ground shall be made level, the rugged places a plain." My own story stands as a strong witness that God's promises are true. When we turn from our own ways and turn to God for healing and direction, amazing things happen.

Pastor Chuck Dollarhide

Every valley shall be lifted up,
and every mountain and hill be made low;
the uneven ground shall become level,
and the rough places plain.
(Isaiah 40:4)

EVERY CHILD OF GOD IS A TREASURE,

BUT I OFTEN FORGET I AM ONE OF THOSE PRECIOUS GEMS.

(Louise Tucker Jones)

I Remember Elvis

Many people still remember and mourn the death of Elvis Presley. I remember and mourn my precious Old English bulldog, Elvis. He was a Christmas gift from my husband, Richard. I will never forget that Christmas. Since we do not have children, Richard makes Christmas a very special occasion for me every year. I started watching the paper in October that year for bulldog puppies. I mentioned to Richard that I would really love to receive one for Christmas. He would acknowledge my request, but since we already had two chows and an American bull terrier I thought the chances of him giving me one were very slim. That Christmas morning I got up to see what Santa Richard had left me. There were several gifts: a dust buster, a key chain, and lots of new clothes. I was pleased and didn't really think about not receiving a new puppy.

As we were leaving for our family Christmas visits, Richard turned to me, "Oh, would you go upstairs and get the box off the table? It's for Ted, I forgot to bring it."

I walked upstairs and picked up the small tin Christmas box. It seemed rather feminine for Ted. As I got back into the car Richard asked, "Did you open it?"

"No," I told him. "You said it was for Ted."

To which he replied, "Open it."

My heart jumped and tears flowed down my face as I saw the picture of a pug-faced, bulldog puppy. He was too young to leave his mother so Richard had given me his picture. My first visit with Elvis was on that Christmas day. I immediately fell in love with him. He was full of mischief, and he fit right into our family. When we were home he had to be with one of us. He was either leaning on a leg or sitting on a foot. Elvis slept right between us every night of his life. He was a faithful, loyal companion.

One Sunday Elvis fell asleep and never woke up. I wasn't home at the time so Richard met me outside to tell me the sad news. The loss was devastating for me. I cried every night because he wasn't there to curl up next to me.

Eventually, I began looking for another bulldog puppy. It took me several weeks to find puppies that came from ancestors with a history of longevity. I had to drive two hundred miles to even look at them. When I arrived, there were thirteen bulldog puppies. One had the exact markings of Elvis.

He won my heart. We have had Gilbert for five years, and just as Elvis did, he blesses us with unconditional love every day. You can't ever replace a love you have lost, but you can be blessed by giving your love away again, unconditionally.

Anitha Ainsworth

Whoever does not love does not know God, for God is love.
(1 John 4:8)

A DOG IS ONE THING ON THIS EARTH
THAT LOVES YOU MORE THAN IT LOVES ITSELF.

From Grief to Gratitude

I thought about her. I dreamed about her. I saw her in every woman I met. Some had her name, Cathy. Others her deep-set blue eyes or her curly hair. Even the slightest resemblance turned my stomach into a knot. Was I never to be free of this woman who had gone after my husband and ultimately married him? The grief and anger drained the life out of me. I tried counseling. I attended recovery workshops. I read books. I screamed into my pillow at night. I was desperate for an end to the pain.

Then one Saturday in 1982 I was drawn to a daylong seminar on the healing power of forgiveness held at a church in my neighborhood. The leader asked us to focus on someone in our lives we had not yet forgiven. My first thought was Cathy. My stomach churned. My head throbbed. How could I forgive such a person? She not only had hurt me but my children too.

Then a voice within gently prodded, "Are you ready to release her?"

I began to shake all over. "Yes, I'm willing," I whispered. I felt certain everyone in the room could hear me. Then something amazing occurred. I simply let go.

I can't describe it. All I know is that for the first time in four years I completely surrendered to the Holy Spirit. I released my grip on Cathy, on my ex-husband, on myself. I stopped grieving—and forgave—just like that.

The following Monday I wrote a letter. The words spilled onto the page without effort. "Dear Cathy," I began. I proceeded to tell her about the seminar and how I learned that my anger had denied both of us the healing power of forgiveness.

On Wednesday afternoon of the same week, the phone rang. There was no mistaking the voice. "Karen? It's Cathy," she said softly. She thanked me for the letter, and acknowledged my courage in writing it. Then she talked briefly of her regret. "If someone had done to me what I did to you," she said, "I don't know if I . . . ever . . . could forgive."

All I had wanted to hear from her, she said that day. As I replaced the receiver, however, I realized that as much as I had welcomed Cathy's words, they paled in comparison to what God was teaching me. He had transformed my human grief into divine gratitude—gratitude for the grace which had changed my life—forever.

I began to see then that no one can hurt me as long as I am in God's hands. Every experience—even the most gut-wrenching—has a divine purpose when I am walking with the Lord.

Karen O'Connor

*For surely I know the plans I have for you,
says the LORD,
plans for your welfare and not for harm,
to give you a future with hope.*
(Jeremiah 29:11)

TO FORGIVE IS TO SET THE PRISONER FREE,
AND THEN DISCOVER THE PRISONER WAS YOU.

Beloved Parent

Beloved parent, now you are
child to me,
As once I was to you,
you will ever be.
God's grace and infinite wisdom unexplained—
As we endure and suffer, stressed and strained.

Caught between the dark and light, sweet one,
Living out your days as when begun—
In innocence sometimes with quiet despair,
Your vacant eyes cast mournful, wistful stares.

And I, your ever-watchful, helpless child,
Search and pray to somehow reconcile

65

How such a life as yours could come to this:
O Heaven, save us, raise us from Abyss.

If patience and tender love like you gave me
Will comfort you and finally set you free,
With roles reversed, I know I'll find the way
To make our lives worth living every day.

Beloved parent, now you are child to me,
And I, your own, lovingly commit to be
Your eyes and ears, mind and memory,
Until God grants us peace in Eternity.

Karen Brantley

Caste all your anxiety on Him,
because He cares for you.
(1 Peter 5:7)

GOD WILL NOT WASTE YOUR PAIN.
(Amy Carmichael)

That Special Christmas

We could hardly wait. We were going to visit Grandma and Grandpa for Christmas. It had been two long years since Dad had been transferred to California. Two difficult years of trying to fit into a new school and make new friends.

The car ride would take the better part of two days, but we were going home. Home to our old neighborhood, friends, and family. Our car was tightly packed with Christmas surprises for aunts, uncles, cousins, and friends. We laughed as we made a "spot" for each of us in the car. There was barely room to sit, let alone spread out for the long ride home.

The excitement kept us all happy and talkative the whole first day.

"Heavy snow," the newsman predicted as we were getting up the following morning. The three of us jumped up and down with glee at the thought of snow forts and sledding. Mom and Dad had looks of trepidation.

"We'd better stop and put on chains," Dad announced when the storm became intense and the roads became slick. When visibility was almost gone, Dad decided it was wiser to stop for the night and begin at first light the following day.

"Don't take much out of the car," Mom said. "Just enough for the night."

It was still dark when dad woke us the next morning. He headed out to warm up the car while we got ready.

The door opened a few minutes later. The look on Dad's face told us that something was terribly wrong.

"We've been robbed," he said. "The entire car has been emptied."

He reached out to hug Mom as she began to cry.

"How could someone do this?" Mom sobbed. "All of our Christmas gifts!"

My heart sank. How could this have happened to us? Didn't they know how long we'd planned this trip? What were they going to do with Grandma's music box or Blair's fire engine?

As more news of the weather came across the television, the decision was made. We couldn't go on. We were going to have to head back. Back to a Christmas without family, gifts, or a tree. Back to a sad reality.

Our hearts were heavy as we turned the car around. The laughter was replaced with crying and complaining. Our thoughts were full of what Christmas might have been.

It was dusk on Christmas Eve when we pulled into our driveway.

"What happened?" asked Mr. Olson, our neighbor. In tearful sobs we shared our shattered dreams and hopes for Christmas.

The house was dark and cold. Our attitudes were somber as we helped empty the car and put away what little was left. Suddenly, the doorbell rang.

"This little tree is looking for a home," announced Mr. Olson dragging a four-foot tree. Behind him were his wife and children, laden with decorations and gifts for under the tree.

"You are so thoughtful," Mom said with tears in her eyes.

The doorbell rang again, and again. Before long we had a refrigerator full of food, we were invited to Christmas dinners and we were surrounded by loving neighbors and friends.

The smell of breakfast woke me the next morning.

"Merry Christmas," Mom and Dad said with a smile.

The fireplace was glowing and the Christmas tree lights sparkled as we gathered to marvel at God's goodness. Who would have ever thought? We had a beautiful tree, wonderful food and presents, good friends, and most importantly—each other.

There were other Christmases with fond memories, but none will ever surpass the cherished holiday memories I hold from that special Christmas.

Margolyn Woods

"You shall love your neighbor as yourself."
(Matthew 22:39b)

A FRIEND WALKS IN WHEN THE REST OF THE WORLD SEEMS TO WALK OUT.

Beautiful Feet

ou don't have to teach children to sing. They begin singing the minute they are born. At least it sounds like singing to a new mother and father. What parent has not sat a little taller in the pew, as their son or daughter sang the solo in a children's choir. Mallory, our youngest child and only daughter, loved to sing. She sang more than she talked, and she talked quite a lot. Mallory demanded center stage with her bright eyes and commanding smile. She drew an audience wherever she went. She loved to perform, acting out her made-up plays or songs on our fireplace hearth, which she used as her stage. She began singing solos for church services and in the church children's programs at a very early age. "She will one day be a talented singer," I proclaimed to family and friends. We started her in voice training and piano lessons to go along with her charismatic personality and God-given talent.

In May of 1995 our children's choir director put together a program consisting of parent and child duets. Mallory and I sang "Beautiful Feet," a song Sandi Patty recorded with her daughter. "How beautiful are the feet of those who carry the good news of Jesus." We spent joyous hours rehearsing together. I still remember her ponytail swinging and her feet tapping as she exuberantly sang the words of her solo part, "Walking with my Savior down a one way street, with my beautiful, beautiful feet." However, as Mallory sang those words we had no idea that in just a few short months, they would become true.

At the beginning of her fourth-grade school year, Mallory began to run a slight fever. A visit to the doctor showed she had the Epstein-Barr virus, or mononucleosis. This normal childhood virus can trigger many serious conditions. In Mallory, it triggered a rare blood disorder, which caused her immune system to turn against her own body. After five days at St. Louis Children's Hospital and many tests, the doctors were able to diagnose the rare condition. A team of doctors took my husband, Darryl, and me into a small room to gently break the news. They began treatment immediately. Nevertheless, by that very night, Mallory was rushed into the Pediatric Intensive Care Unit, where she slipped into a coma. After eight days on complete life support, the Lord promoted Mallory to heaven—on November 22, 1995, at the age of nine.

We now know that most children with Mallory's condition do not live past the age of three. God was so gracious to give us nine precious years with her—years filled with laughter and love.

We have many wonderful memories of Mallory, which are treasures and a comfort as we reflect on them now that she is gone. We have a videotape of our performance singing "Beautiful Feet," which brings joy and laughter, as well as tears each time we watch it. Nothing comforts me more than to envision her walking with her Savior down that one-way street with her beautiful, beautiful feet.

Teresa Griggs

Praise the Lord, for the Lord is good;
sing to His name, for He is gracious.
(Psalm 135:3)

DEATH IS NOT A PERIOD BUT A COMMA
IN THE LIFE OF ONE WHO FOLLOWS CHRIST.

Never Alone

I had been dragged kicking and screaming from a town where I knew everyone, to a city where I knew no one. We couldn't find a church, I couldn't find a Christian Women's Club, and I had no friends. There was no one to talk to except the milkman, and he eventually got so nervous he started rolling the bottles in by the driveway. I was also pregnant with my fifth child. All in all, life was quite depressing.

One Sunday my husband got our other four ready for church. (If you see him in heaven with an extra star in his crown, that will be why.) Four children ready for church only lasts a very short time, but Bill took the half-minute before disaster struck to see if I was ready. I was not.

I was sitting in my nightie in the middle of the bed waiting for everyone to be out of sight, out of sound, and out of my orbit.

"Aren't you going to church this morning?" asked my husband.

I folded my fat little arms on my fat little stomach and announced that I certainly was not, and could he please take the children and go, go, go (all in loving tones, of course). My lower lip was stuck out so far you could have ridden to town on it.

He disappeared down the hall. In dejected silence, I said to myself, "Well, now he's gone and left me." Women *do* tend to be a little irrational at times. Life suddenly seemed unbearable. The loving care of my husband was dismissed, as was the idea that this situation was really only temporary.

I was a fairly new Christian, but I was under the impression that God probably had not followed me to this place of gloom. I had given up reading my Bible and attending Bible studies. In reality, I had let go of God. If I could have thought of a way to commit suicide that required no energy, for I was tired to the bone, I would surely have done it.

But do you know what? God never lets go of one of His children, no matter how insipid their thoughts or actions. I learned a wonderful lesson of the faithfulness of God, and will always remember it. We are the sheep of His pasture, and He has never lost a single one. That day, I turned back to Him and He reached down and picked me up. He reminded me that I was never alone. He accepted me just as I was: turned from Him, despondent, and full of self.

Cid Davidson

God is faithful; by Him you were called into the fellowship of His Son, Jesus Christ our Lord.

(1 Corinthians 1:9)

HE WHO LOSES MONEY LOSES MUCH.

HE WHO LOSES A FRIEND LOSES MORE.

HE WHO LOSES FAITH LOSES ALL.

A Dollar's Worth of Patriotism

*T*rushed into the shop just twenty minutes before closing, remembering a basket of red, white, and blue ribbons for sale on the counter near the cashier. I wanted our family to wear them to church the next day, but when I neared the counter I saw that the basket was empty. I mentally reprimanded myself for not buying them earlier and asked if they had more ribbons someplace else. "No," the clerk answered. My face must have mirrored my disappointment.

"How many did you need?" she asked.

"Three," I said without further explanation. Somehow in the five days since the terrorist attack on the United States, no one needed explanations for anything. It was perfectly all right to cry over the phone or in public places. People understood when you lost your train of thought and it didn't seem important anyway, because we all had the same things on our minds.

I had sat transfixed in front of the TV since that Tuesday, still unable to believe the scenes played out before me. Planes exploding. Buildings burning and crumbling. In a very brief span of time, thousands of people died. It was impossible to comprehend. I had already attended two prayer services. My husband, son, and I had gone to the church and prayed together—just the three of us—but the emotional pain was still raw and I often found myself in tears.

"I'll make you some ribbons," the clerk said gently. Surprised, yet thankful, I followed her to the floral counter where she pulled out rolls of shiny red, white and blue metallic ribbon. Not knowing what else to say while she measured and cut meticulously I asked the price of the ribbons.

"Twenty-five cents."

Only a quarter! I was shocked. "Then make me four," I quickly added. I could at least spend a dollar on the patriotic symbols. *A dollar's worth of patriotism,* I thought cynically. Isn't that what we want most of the time? Certainly we are not among the lot who burn the flag, defame it, and take freedom where it was never meant to go, thereby violating other people's rights and beliefs. No, we aren't among the infidels who use God's name in vain or blasphemous ways rather than in worship and praise, but we are guilty of complacency.

We want a little patriotism, not a lot. We will salute the flag at public gatherings, "rah-rah" the president if he says what we want, sing the national anthem at baseball games, vote if it's convenient, wave miniature, plastic flags at Fourth of July parades, and "ooh and ahh" the fireworks that portray "Old Glory" waving. We even use the freedom of press to write critical letters about our leaders. But how often do we get on our knees and thank God for that precious freedom? How many of us pray for the president and government officials as the Bible commands? And far too often the old cliché "crooked politician" finds its way into our vocabulary when, in truth, numerous godly people are serving our country. Even prayer lost its place in the public realm, but now . . . well, now we are all praying. God is mentioned on the public airways. Prayer vigils are televised. The nation is encouraged to pray by a Bible-believing, Christian president.

The clerk interrupted my thoughts with "Be right back," and ran to another part of the store to get more ribbon. When she returned we chatted amiably. No, she didn't know anyone in the buildings or planes. Nor did I, but my child-care worker had a cousin missing. He was attending a meeting on the one hundred and sixth floor of the World Trade Center.

"I'm sorry," she said.

So was I. I didn't even know him. I didn't know any of the people on the four planes or in the buildings or on the streets. I didn't know the rescue workers who were buried alive trying to save others, yet I hurt for their families. I was sorry for all of them. I was also sorry for a nation in mourning. A senseless act of violence. Wives without husbands, husbands without wives. Parents without children, children without parents. Brothers, sisters, friends. Gone forever.

The girl handed me the ribbons and I carried the small bundle as gently as if it were a china cup, not wanting to squash the precious contents inside. The next morning my husband, son, and I donned the patriotic symbols on our lapels, adding an angel in the middle, and attended church, where we prayed with countless others that God would intervene and save our country. Heal our land. We continue praying that He will give us a righteous courage to face our enemies with Him in command. And with the world watching we proudly pray, sing, and plead, "God bless America!"

⌐⌐◠ *Louise Tucker Jones*

Let the wise also hear and gain in learning.
(Proverbs 1:5a)

To GROW TALL SPIRITUALLY,
A MAN MUST FIRST LEARN TO KNEEL.

Time

Those who know say
    this pain will ease,
I have no choice
    but to wait and grieve.

My mind knows for sure it was best that you go,
But the journey from my head to my heart is slow.

The warmth of your touch on a blustery day,
The love and kindness in the words you did say.

Sitting in silence in each other's embrace,
The love of a lifetime shown plain on my face.

It is to these memories that I desperately cling,
Waiting for the calm that time will bring.

Free from the pain that tormented you here,
The prospect of death you never did fear.

Released from this world into heaven you went,
Christ's waiting arms is where you were sent.

The comfort of life without sorrow or pain,
Eternity with your Savior is what you did gain.

Knowledge of grace was the strength you did need,
Good deeds on the earth was no case to plead.

In that same grace I find the will to go on,
Trusting the sorrow will soon be gone.

The wedding vows said till death do us part,
But not even death takes your love from my heart.

So when you look down from heaven above,
I want to say thanks for a lifetime of love.

Joe Walstad

*Weeping may linger for the night,
but joy comes with the morning.* (Psalm 30:5)

WHEN IT RAINS. . . . IT POURS GOD'S GRACE.

Angels on Earth

*T*lay very still beside my husband of twelve years and stared at the ceiling. Frozen with anxiety and foreboding, I wondered who this stranger was, lying close beside me in the darkness. I sensed that he, too, was wide awake, staring silently and coldly away from me.

"Is there someone else in this marriage with us?" I heard myself say.

The anger and defensiveness in his tone of voice as he shot back, "I don't have to answer that," spoke volumes. He had been having an affair. My comfortable, happy, secure world came crashing down all around me.

The next few minutes are vivid in my memory. I quietly dressed and tiptoed downstairs and out the front door. I began to run in the predawn darkness, down the residential street to a wide-open country field. A fine mist started to fall and blended in with the tears streaming down my cheeks. I was wracked with panic as thoughts raced through my mind. What had I done wrong? What was I going to do?

Fear and unbearable anguish pressed in from every side. Then, I remembered a faint voice from my childhood. It was my adored grandmother, sitting by her fireplace, Bible opened in her lap. "God will never leave you nor forsake you," she had said. Through my anguish, I looked up through the rain and talked to God. "Please help me. I don't know what to do. I am terrified. I have three little children depending on me and I am so frightened. Please God, give me strength." I ran on and on, and as I prayed, the overwhelming anguish and panic began to fall away. I didn't feel so all-alone. The sky brightened with the sunrise and, exhausted, I turned back toward home.

Quietly I opened the door to the sound of the sweetest little voice I have ever heard. It was the sleepy voice of my baby boy, standing in his diaper at the top of the stairs. The sun's rays were glinting all around him. With his little arms outstretched, he cried, "Mommy, Mommy." I bounded up the stairs, pulled his sweet little body close and felt his soft, precious arms encircle my neck. In that moment, feeling the trust and love of my baby, God's presence and goodness enveloped me. I thought, "I will always be a mommy. I have the love and devotion of my three precious children. I am not alone. No matter what the future may hold, God will always be with me. He will provide the strength to get through this."

For the next four years I was embroiled in a vicious court battle for custody of my children. The threat of losing my children was unrelenting and terrifying. I fought to hold myself together; to go to work every day, to be a good mother to my children who continued to reside temporarily with me. On many nights, long after my children were asleep, I would lie wide awake asking God to help me.

God answered my prayers through a wonderful network of family, friends, and strangers. Their "random acts of kindness" soothed my aching soul and gave the emotional "manna" I needed to survive each day. During the darkest days of the custody trial my coworkers sent notes of encouragement and brought meals to my home. When I had to face weeks of intimidating court proceedings, my mother and three sisters took off work to be with me. When my children had no home, my elderly mother let us crowd into her small, rented house. After many long and costly court hearings and numerous appeals I was awarded custody of my children.

The hundreds of kindnesses of family and friends helped me shoulder the burden of that difficult time in my life. Innumerable times, strangers reached out to me just when I felt I was at the end of my rope.

At one point during my long ordeal, someone said to me, "Lori, at the end of this experience you will find rooms in your heart you did not know were there."

I now understand that remark. For the rest of my life I will remember the days I felt so vulnerable and crushed beneath the inequities of the legal system. I will remember the difference it made in my life when people were kind to me. Through this long and dark period of my life, God was always with me. He was with me in the form of angels on earth, my family and friends, and sometimes strangers, whose hands reached out to steady me and catch me when I began to fall.

Nowadays, as people cross my path, I go out of my way to smile, to be warm, friendly, and helpful. We never know who might need to be treated with an extra touch of kindness and consideration. I have become a better person because of my ordeal. I know what true love is. I know God loves me. My children are well on their way to growing up and making their own way in life. I hope I have taught them the same lessons I have learned. God asks us to be angels on earth to those who are hurting, lonely, or in need. And God is always with us, often, through the kindness of our fellow man.

Lori Pettus

I give thanks to my God always for you because of the grace of God that has been given you in Christ Jesus.
(1 Corinthians 1:4)

KINDNESS IS VERY HARD TO GIVE AWAY; IT KEEPS COMING BACK TO YOU.

Sprinkled with Love

Mom's Apple Pie

Preheat oven to 400 degrees

Pastry

    1–1/4 cups all-purpose
      flour
    1/2 teaspoon salt
    1/4 cup shortening
    4 tablespoons cold water

Apple Filling

    2–2/3 pounds Granny Smith apples,
      pared, cored, and thinly sliced
    1/4 cup granulated sugar
    1/4 cup brown sugar
    2 Tablespoons flour

Combine apples, sugars, and flour in large bowl.

Prepare pastry. Stir together flour and salt in medium bowl. Cut in shortening. Stir in water. Roll pastry on lightly floured surface. Put 11-inch rolled dough in pie pan. Pour in apple mixture. Cover with second rolled dough, overlapping edges. Crimp. Trim. (Give daughter extra dough!) Bake at 400 degrees for 15 minutes, then at 350 degrees for 45 minutes. Cool for 15 minutes and enjoy!

At the tender age of five, I stood on my tiptoes, my hands resting on top of the kitchen counter. I stared at the pie dough my mother was preparing. She was making her famous apple pie. A large bowl of apples sat to the side. Sprinkles of flour covered the piece of wax paper, as she rolled out the pie dough with the side of the twelve-ounce glass tumbler. I loved to watch my mother make pies. I knew if I stood there long enough, my mother would pinch off pieces of dough and give them to me. She would make enough dough for two crusts, one for the top and one for the bottom. There was always extra dough left, just for me!

I would take the dough in my hands, roll it into a ball, and pop in into my mouth. "Not too much, or you will get a stom-achache," she would say, giving me fair warning.

That was many years ago. To this day, when I make an apple pie, I still use the same recipe. The page is torn and spotted with stains, yet alive with memories. When I find myself slicing the apples, and making two crusts, one for the top and one for the bottom, I always seem to have plenty of dough left. Perhaps enough to sneak a bite or two, roll it into a ball, and pop it into my mouth. Is there any doubt? Some things never change, like apple pie and the little kid in all of us.

My mother passed away two years ago. I miss the days of sharing moments with her, but I will always have the precious memories that we shared. Her apple pie tradition was passed on to me. I find myself preparing apple pie the same way she did, as my three children stand close by, standing on their tiptoes, with outstretched arms, waiting for pieces of dough to come their way.

To this day, when I smell the aroma of freshly baked apple pie, I recall the precious memories of my mother. A big thank-you to all of the mothers who share bits of their lives and set their own traditions with their children.

— *Vickie Jenkins*

Train your children in the right way,
and when they are old, they will not stray.
(Proverbs 22:6)

TRADITION IS A GIFT WE GIVE OUR CHILDREN AND THEIR CHILDREN AND THEIR CHILDREN AND. . . .

Empty Nest, Full Heart

Where once a family stood, now I stand alone. It is not from any great tragedy but from a job well done. My children are adults and now travel on a journey of their own. One is a teacher and mother; one is a scholar, studying in Europe; and one has a career which led him far from our home. As a mother, my greatest goal was to raise well-adjusted, successful children, to help them become strong and independent adults. I did that. Now they are gone. After twenty-six years of motherhood, more than half of my life, I now wonder what I am supposed to do.

I remember the years of cooking, carpools, soccer practice, and homework projects when I could only dream of a free moment for myself. Now I long for those slumber parties that kept me awake all night and even find myself missing the arguments in the backseat of the car while I am driving. Most of all, I miss how much I was needed. The free moments for which I dreamed now seem to be all I have. I feel so alone.

Deep in my heart, however, I know I am not alone. God has always been with me. He gave me strength and made my family strong. Now, as I face the challenge of this new chapter in my life I know He is with me. Although I count my children as precious gifts from God, I realize they are not His greatest gift to me. His never-ending love is His greatest gift.

Though my children are grown and gone, my mission continues. With God beside me, I find new purposes and travel on. My life is different now, full in a new way.

His love lifts me up and gives me the strength to do new things with my life. I once read that there is a test to find out if your mission on earth is finished: If you're alive, it isn't!

Maureen MacLellan

Now faith is the assurance of things hoped for,
the conviction of things not seen.
(Hebrews 11:1)

HAVE THY TOOLS READY, GOD WILL FIND THEE WORK.

Journey to Forgiveness

"Your father has died. . . ."

"Where was he?" I asked.

"He was alone," came the reply from the other end of the phone.

"How did it happen?" I questioned.

Silence, then the reply: "Of his own hand."

A flood of conflicting emotions collided to drown me. All the stages of grief were coming at me rapid-fire and in illogical sequence. But what is logical when your father has just killed himself?

Perhaps the caller was confused; someone must have murdered him. Maybe he was robbed and then murdered.

He left a note, "Call my sister."

What about his son?

My parents divorced when I was only five years old. Then dad disappeared for the next eight years. He basically abandoned us. He was a stranger to the point that I didn't even recognize him when we reunited. But the hurt was there and could never be repaired. He had never been involved in my life: my scouting events, my sporting events, my commissioning, my graduation, or my wedding. Now, at age thirty-two, I felt the ultimate abandonment inflicted upon me by my father.

The shock, the horror, the reality, the flood of emotions were all too great to deal with. The obligatory requirements were met. The funeral arrangements were made. The hours of conversations with strangers seemed never-ending and even tortuous. As the furniture was hauled out and loaded into the U-Haul, the details of the scene were indelibly etched in my mind. I would love to erase images of the bullet hole in the recliner, the drops of blood on the floor, the floodlights illuminating the backyard in a surreal fashion as the dogs ran loose.

The fact that we travel this way but once and are the sum total of our choices hit home with me that week. What were my choices? Had I wasted any of my life? At age sixty-five, what would I see looking back? Would I be proud of my life? Would I have made a difference? How would my children remember me? Was I a good husband and father?

The grieving process lasted about three years. Anger, denial, regret, and finally acceptance were all emotions I felt. The opportunities to have a relationship with my earthly father died when he pulled the trigger. It was his choice. I can't change that. My hope for the future must be my Heavenly Father. He is the one who is unchanging. He is the one there for me day in and day out. He is the one who has a future prepared for me. Through prayer and the passage of time He has shown me how to cope with my father's death.

My grief journey brought me to forgiveness. I have forgiven my father for his actions against me, whether intentional or not. It has been the road to fulfillment, the road to health, and the road to true happiness.

Mike Ozment

Now may the Lord of peace Himself give you peace at all times in all ways.
(2 Thessalonians 3:16a)

FORGIVENESS WARMS THE HEART AND COOLS THE STING.

The Gift of a Song

*I*t promised to be a hard winter in Sudburg. Trees and ground stared stark and bare during dark and long days. Farmers fretted about their crops, hoping against bleak hope for a good crop next year.

It was a wedding day in the little burg for old bachelor Benjamin Bowen and young Simone. The town folk witnessed the tying of the wedlock knot at the village church then went to salute the newlyweds at Muller's Inn, all hoping to find merriment to distract them from their mounting troubles. Just as the glasses were raised for a toast, a storm set in with howling wind and rain so heavy that no one could leave the inn.

"I wouldn't put my mare out in this storm," said one. "She skitters when she hears thunder." All agreed they would have to stay put until the storm passed. Mothers gathered the youngest ones close as each shudder of thunder and bright shiver of lightning surprised the sky. Older children gathered near their mamas, playing peek-a-boo and tying Moses' baskets in hand-kerchiefs to distract the babies from the wiles of the storm. The men stood close to the bar, jesting and boasting, spouting plans of big yields from their poor acres.

Each patron of the inn that day did not discuss the deep worries they carried just under the surface of the conversation. When they ran out of things to say, the sounds of the storm filled the silence.

By ten o'clock the howling gale had not abated, so Mrs. Muller gathered blankets and arranged the tables to give a comfortable night to her guests. Wee ones had just tumbled off to slumber land when a great gust blew open the door and deposited a bedraggled stranger inside. Two men ran to close the wooden door, straining against the force of the gale, until the latch was locked.

"Give 'im some room by the fireside," ordered Mrs. Muller. "I'll serve up some stew. Now who will loan the man a dry cloak?" she said, looking for a volunteer. Seeing a stringed instrument strapped under his cloak, she asked, "You've an instrument—a violin? Maybe you could give us some music," she went on. The poor drenched, weather-besotted man only nodded his head.

The traveler heard the woeful music sung by the heart of each one in the room. He heard the bride's wish-filled cry that her husband would always love her, for she knew she was no prize.

The priest sang that he had no hope to give, as he, too, needed that commodity. Mrs. Muller sang of a forgetful husband. She feared losing the inn. He heard a wife mourn the loss of a babe. Another grieved about a disobedient son. The sadness of the songs pressed hard on the stranger whose empathizing heart grew heavy.

"What is your trade?" asked a man, interrupting the stranger's thoughts.

"I am a troubadour, bard, balladeer."

"Sing us a song, then," someone requested.

"Not just now," he answered. "In a little while I will play my mandolin."

The folk talked into the night and some drifted off to sleep, but none heard a tune from the singer with the mandolin. At just about three in the morning, when each eye had closed save those of the bard, he picked up his mandolin and started a soft, soothing song. The balladeer moved through the room, sensing the song coursing in each heart, as among them he moved along. To the weary farmers whose pockets were nearly empty, he sang of good weather and a bountiful crop next year. He sang a song of assurance to the new bride, told another that her inner beauty would be recognized by a worthy man. He sang to Mrs. Muller that she shouldn't worry over her husband's forgetfulness, that no ill would befall her. He chanted to the woman who lamented for her lost newborn that she would give birth to several more children in the coming years. The troubadour advised a young woman to develop her mind and soul, to not rely solely on her beauty. To a young man he chanted not to worry, for his future looked fine indeed. He sang a song to a baby that her talents were remarkable and would make her the pride of the town. To the mother whose son caused much grief, he assured her the son would reform.

For about two hours he sang soft lullabies, comforting, encouraging the slumbering villagers. The rain tittered lightly upon the roof, the wild gusts calmed, and peace entered the souls of the sleeping inn guests.

Ere the first blush of dawn painted the sky, the traveler was gone. He'd paid his bill with the songs he had sung and left for the next day's town.

When the villagers woke in the dim Muller's Inn, they remarked of a beautiful dream with fields yielding much. They all had good luck and no worries dimmed their hope.

"I heard the troubadour playing a song, like he knew what I needed to hear. I sensed him bending down singing in my ear."

"Where has he gone? Was he just a dream?" each person asked another.

No sign of him remained, but through the years spanning that time and now, his songs resound in Sudburg: don't be sad, be confident, think of good things, not sad, encourage each other, help carry each load, let not your fellow fall.

They all seemed to recall the troubadour's final song, singing, "I'll be back in Sudburg someday. As long as love is alive, there is plenty of reason to sing. Hear the songs you sing to yourselves, and help each other to sing. If you see someone who can't find his tune, hum a few bars, 'til he catches on."

The villagers all felt a glow of relief, an omen of good things to come. No one grieved and all felt relieved in the opening of that new dawn. The wind had abated, the morn was bright, and the troubadour plodded on.

Rebecca Marshall Farnbach

*May the God of hope fill you with all joy and peace
in believing, so that you may abound in hope
by the power of the Holy Spirit.*
(Romans 15:13)

PEACE IS NOT THE ABSENCE OF TROUBLE BUT THE PRESENCE OF GOD.

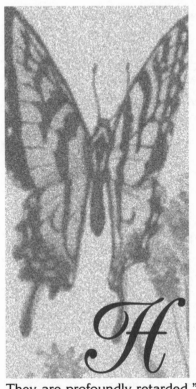

Through God's Eyes

His words tore my heart: "Mrs. Costilow, as an experienced psychologist, my advice is to institutionalize Kelly and Kevin. They are profoundly retarded." I ran out of the psychologist's office crying uncontrollably. The words kept resounding in my ears as I drove home. How could I face this? Desperate thoughts ran through my mind; don't go home, just run away, drive into the brick wall, end it all. This was too much to bear. I loved my twin sons dearly, but I just couldn't deal with this news!

When I pulled into the driveway, I noticed my friend's car. "Irene, I don't know why I'm here. God just told me to come and wait for you." She was an angel sent by God. I collapsed into her arms and cried on her shoulder for hours. She tried to reassure

me: "Somehow, God will help you and see you through this."
I wasn't sure I believed her.

I didn't handle Kelly and Kevin's situation very well. I was depressed and lonely, often shaking my fist at God. I was also angry, grieving the death of a dream for my children's perfect life. For days I would sit in my old, comfy chair and ask God, "Why?"

During this time, God spoke to my heart and reminded me how much He loved His Son, Jesus. It hurt Him to see His Son suffer and die. I began to realize that God understood my pain and heartache. And, I realized that I couldn't do this alone. I needed God to help me through all of this.

The Bible says that God gave His Son, Jesus, to die on the cross for my sins. He then rose from the dead and lives at the right hand of God today. He died for me! All I had to do was ask Him to forgive my sins and to be a part of my life.

Although, I'd heard this before, I'd never really thought this applied to me because I was a "good person." However, God gently guided me to see my need for Him, not only in my circumstance but in my life. Finally, I prayed and asked God to forgive my sins, come into my life and to help me with Kelly and Kevin.

After I prayed, I fully expected a miracle—that God would "fix Kelly and Kevin."

I kept watching and waiting for signs of improvement, but nothing changed! Their needs remained the same.

I was in for a big surprise because I noticed that I was the one changing. My attitude became one of patience and acceptance. I began seeing Kelly and Kevin as the most precious gifts that God could have given to me. They are the reason I found Jesus. I'll forever be thankful. God doesn't make mistakes. He knew what He was doing when He chose to give these special boys to me.

The Bible says: "If anyone be in Christ, he is a new creation, old things are passed away and all things have become new." That is what happened to me! As a new creation in Christ, I began to see Kelly and Kevin with new eyes . . . God's eyes.

Irene Costilow

The name of the Lord is a strong tower;
the righteous run into it and are safe.
(Proverbs 18:10)

REMEMBER, SOME OF GOD'S GREATEST GIFTS
ARE UNANSWERED PRAYERS.

A Blessing a Day

t was a warm June day and I was feeling especially low. My marriage had been on a downhill slide and trying to put things back together was draining me physically and emotionally. I was reflecting on life over the last ten years of our marriage and wondering what had happened to the couple who had such hopes and dreams. We were going to conquer the world together, and now it looked as though the world had conquered us.

I began to pray and seek the Lord's wisdom for direction, comfort, and strength. I asked for hope and encouragement to pull my life back together. One afternoon I turned on the radio just in time to hear one of my favorite songs. It spoke about a childlike faith and the anticipation of exciting things to come.

I was comforted. Was the song a coincidence? Does God comfort us through songs on the radio?

The next day a friend brought over a loaf of her special sourdough bread along with the ingredients to make more loaves. She explained how making bread could be therapeutic.

"After all," she said, "you have to pound it before making it into a beautiful loaf."

I was once again comforted. Was this a coincidence or was God comforting me through a friend?

Day after day God sent me special blessings. Sometimes it came in the form of a song, a loaf of bread, a beautiful sunrise or sunset, the call of a meadowlark or the laughter from one of my children. As I began to look for my special blessings sent from the Lord, my hurting heart began to heal and grief began to loosen its grip.

We worked through that difficult season in our marriage and God brought us into a deeper and richer understanding of love and forgiveness. Reflecting back on all God had done in my hour of despair, I began to thank him for the special blessings He had been so gracious to share with me. These daily blessings lifted me above my circumstances and gave me hope. He promises to do this for all of His children if we will only tune our hearts and listen to the words He speaks through His creation.

What is your blessing for today? Maybe it is reading this inspirational story or maybe it's passing it on to a friend who's grieving a loss. For me, today's blessing is sharing this simple story of the love of God. He reaches down into hurting hearts and gives rays of sunshine during dark cloudy days. Grief may have its grip on our emotions, but God grips us with his love and longs to ease our grief with a blessing a day.

Gayle Team-Smith

The Lord has done great things for us, and we rejoice.
(Psalm 126:3)

Simple blessings can break the cycle of grief.

When Prodigals Don't Return

s my husband and I sat in the judge's chambers finalizing the adoption of our four-year-old daughter, the word "prodigal" was not in my vocabulary. Holding Paula on my lap, I pictured her bursting through the door after school to tell me about her day over milk and cookies. I even imagined how sweet and beautiful she would be at sixteen.

However, by the time Paula actually reached her sixteenth birthday, I had been inside more judges' chambers and juvenile courtrooms than I cared to count. "Pick-up notices" were a way of life as Paula ran away from home again and again. I wondered how this could happen. We were good people. We went to church, school programs, and took family vacations. We loved Paula! But, sometimes love isn't enough. Children have a free will and make choices concerning behavior. After praying and crying until there were no more tears, I finally released my daughter to our Heavenly Father.

The pain didn't end. In fact, it increased. People blamed us for her behavior. After all, how could we be good parents if our child left home? Yet God understood and comforted us through His Word as no one else could. Psalm 34:18 says: "The Lord is close to those whose hearts are breaking." Only God knew how much my heart was hurting. He even collects and treasures all my tears.

Paula is still a prodigal, but no longer mine. She is now God's prodigal, and when she finally decides to come home, all of heaven will rejoice!

Louise Tucker Jones

"*My grace is sufficient for you,*
for power is made perfect in weakness."
(2 Corinthians 12:9–10)

A LABOR OF LOVE IS NEVER LOST IN HEAVEN'S EYES.

Eternal Hope

"Where's my mommy?" my two-year-old sister Hope asked innumerable times after the death of our mother. It was the most heart-wrenching question to answer. We would tell her mommy was in heaven. Hope would then want to get on an airplane and go there. It tore us up.

Losing a mother at a young age is a life-changing event. It can be devastating to a family, I know. I've always felt that a mother is the glue that holds a family together. When that bond is taken away there is a void that no other person on earth can fill. No matter how hard they try.

We were a family of six, a country family who had the world by the tail, when at the age of forty-four mom was diagnosed with breast cancer. She had just had a baby, very unexpectedly, the year before. Our family was the happiest it had ever been!

We prayed so hard that the Lord would heal her and we had the faith that He would. He did, but not in the way we expected. It really was a win-win situation either way for mom. Either be healed in a physical way on earth or the grandest way of all, eternally. God chose eternally.

Recently, with the terrible events of the World Trade Center, the grief we felt at losing a parent has been brought into sharp focus again to us. These many children who lost parents need the prayers of all Christians to get them through their grief.

Grief doesn't end after a couple of months. As I got older, many things would bring it into focus again for me—a graduation, a wedding, and especially the birth of a child. That's when I would miss my mom so tremendously. I would ache. I wanted so much for her to be there with me, sharing in my happiness. But you know what? She was. I didn't see her presence, but I certainly felt it.

Hope, just like my sister's name, is a precious gift. We had the hope that the Lord would heal mom. Now we have the hope of seeing mom again someday. My sisters and I often talk about that grand reunion in heaven. We long for the hugs we know are coming when we walk through those gates into the arms of our mother.

Bonnie Morgan

So that we, who were the first to set our hope on Christ, might live for the praise of His glory. (Ephesians 1:12)

IN ALL THINGS, GIVE PRAISE TO GOD.

My Sister, My Friend

I was really mean to my sister growing up. It wasn't intentional. It was just that I was the popular one—cute, slender and athletic—and she was chunky and shy. She never had much self-confidence, most likely because she was always in my shadow. Life wasn't easy on Linda, and neither was I. Looking back, it's hard to believe that Linda was ever nice to me, because I sure tried to push her away.

After college, I continued to have everything go my way. I lived in Hawaii, became a court reporter, and lived the life of a professional. Then I met a wonderful man and got married.

Meanwhile, Linda's life was falling apart. She got married, but soon found herself a single mom supporting her son. She became depressed and turned to marijuana for relief.

Marijuana! I was disgusted with her. I couldn't believe that she would resort to using drugs when she had a child. I treated her terribly, refusing to be around her. I had no compassion. I was extremely judgmental, as I had been her entire life. Now, I not only preached to her about how to get her life in order, I had all of the answers on how she should raise her son, too.

Our lives grew apart and our relationship became strained. But it was never completely severed, because Linda continued to call and keep in touch. She had so many reasons to be angry with me, but she never was. Meanwhile, I had two normal, healthy children. Boy, I wish I'd had these kids back when I had all of the answers to Linda's parenting shortcomings. All of a sudden, I realized that life wasn't as easy as I thought. Children, and a normal, healthy marriage, with its ups and downs, gave me a big dose of reality.

I was trying to hold on to a career, be a good wife and mother . . . and I wasn't doing any of them very well. I was incredibly stretched and stressed.

Now I was the one who needed my sister. I needed to talk with someone who was nonjudgmental and with whom I could safely share my problems. She was there for me. All of a sudden, being slender and popular didn't matter to me anymore. Linda didn't hold the years of haughtiness over my head. She loved me unconditionally, and stuck with me through some difficult times.

Obviously, the older we get the wiser we get. I wasn't a very good sister to Linda. I wasn't very thoughtful or loving to the only sister I have. I grieve for the many years I wasn't there for her. My goal now is to return the unconditional love she's always shown me.

— Anonymous

Beloved, since God loved us so much,
we also ought to love one another.
(1 John 4:11)

AN ERROR DOESN'T BECOME A MISTAKE

UNTIL YOU REFUSE TO CORRECT IT.

A Two-Minute Journey

T died while in labor with my second son. On the surface, that seems like a bad thing, but the doctors and nurses revived me after two minutes, and the experience changed my life forever.

Many people want to know where I went during those two minutes. I enjoy telling them, but I never realized the impact it could have until I told Kathy. I'd been going to the same Denny's restaurant for breakfast for three years and Kathy was my favorite waitress. She had a warm and bubbly personality, and I always tried to sit in her section.

One day Kathy seemed forgetful and not her usual happy self. When I asked her what was wrong, she burst into tears and told me her ex-husband (a former drug addict) had overdosed and was in a coma in the hospital. Even though they had been divorced for over five years, Kathy still loved him. She left him to protect herself and her two daughters, who were now sixteen and twenty. The girls were terribly upset about their father.

I had barely finished saying "I'm really sorry" when the story of when I died suddenly poured out of my mouth. I told Kathy that when I died, all my pain and worries just disappeared and I felt totally at peace for the first time in my life. As life left my body, the room dimmed to a pinpoint of light, with all sounds and feelings folding in with the darkness until I was cocooned in tranquillity. Then I started advancing toward the light. The more I traveled, the warmer and happier I became. A thought bloomed in my being—I was going home.

Then I was suddenly wrenched away. A harsh voice next to my head boomed, "Doctor, we have a pulse!" Someone pried my right eye open and a bright, painful light slammed into my skull. I pulled away from the hand and started to fight the people around me. I was furious! "Why?" I muttered. Why did they take me from the light? How could they have brought me back to such a cold, sterile environment?

Another voice next to my head said, "You're okay. Your baby's okay. Everything will be fine." My baby! Thoughts of my unborn baby and my eighteen-month-old son made me want to stay. My consciousness returned and an hour later I delivered my ten pound son by C-section. But I will never forget my two-minute journey and how it changed my life. I have plenty to live for, but I'm not afraid of death anymore. I know that when my adventures here are through and I've done all I need to do, something wonderful awaits me.

When I finished my story, I told Kathy I believed her ex-husband had gone through many trials and tribulations. Perhaps it was time for him to be rewarded with that which I had just gotten a glimpse.

Kathy was absent from work for a week. The first day I saw her after her return she rushed over to hug me. "I told my daughters what you told me," she said. "The day their father died, we were all sitting beside his bed holding his hands recounting our favorite memories of him. When he passed away we cried, but it was different from the crying we'd done before your story. Now, we cried because we would miss him, but we didn't cry for him." Kathy's eyes brimmed with tears and she hugged me again before she continued. "Because of what you went through, we all visualized his journey as his long-deserved peace."

I find it amazing that a traumatic episode in my life could help not only me but others as well. I was happy I could help someone, but that day with Kathy I learned yet another lesson from my ordeal so many years ago. Life is a voyage in which we all keep each other afloat. But no matter how rocky or wonderful the trip, the final destination is well worth the wait.

Pam Drummond

For God so loved the world He gave His only Son,
so that everyone who believes in Him may not perish
but may have eternal life.
(John 3:16)

WITNESS GOD'S PROMISES,
THEN WATCH HIM WORK MIRACLES.

Beside Still Waters

*L*ess than a year after suffering a twelve-week miscarriage, I discovered I was pregnant again. Things went well with this second pregnancy until approximately one week before my due date when my obstetrician failed to pick up the fetal heartbeat.

All that night I asked God to let me feel something, the slightest movement, anything to let me know that the baby was going to be all right.

But all I felt was stillness.

The next morning, plans were finalized for labor to be induced that day.

Once admitted, I was taken to the maternity ward where labor was induced. For the rest of the day and into the night we listened to the silence of the fetal monitor. The pain that silence brought was worse than the contractions.

In the early morning hours, after what seemed an eternity of hoping against hope, I delivered a ten-pound two-ounce stillborn son.

For the next three days, I lay in the maternity ward listening to the babies down the hall. I turned away uninformed photographers who came to my room asking if I wanted pictures taken of my baby. I was making burial plans.

Once home, it wasn't any easier walking by the nursery night after night, seeing the empty crib and still toys, but my husband and I never gave up hope that someday God would bless us with a family.

We began applying at every adoption agency we could find, but most of them had waiting lists longer than the Congressional Record. There was nothing for us to do but add our names and wait.

After several years and still no word, we decided to take a giant step of faith. We sold our memory-filled two-bedroom home and bought a four-bedroom house instead. We were trusting that one day God would fill up those bedrooms.

Yet when I telephoned the adoption agencies to give them our new address, I was informed by several of them that since our move had taken us out of the county, we could no longer remain on their adoption list.

We were stunned. Our hopes were crashing and burning before our eyes. Our church was having special services all that week, but I didn't feel like going to any of them. Mother's Day had just passed, and I was in no mood to listen to some preacher tell me how much God loves me.

Instead of going to church, my husband and I decided to stay home and continue unpacking. We had been in our new home one week and were still in wall-to-wall boxes. Figuring it would be the easiest room to arrange, we decided to unpack the nursery. It seemed a bit futile to spend so much time arranging a room that wasn't being used by anyone, but we were compelled to finish.

Russ kept at it until about midnight. He had to go to work early the next day, so I stayed up to complete the job, even though I ended up doing more crying than unpacking.

It wasn't fair. None of this was fair. But after a few more hours of licking my wounds and being mad at God, I finally surrendered. God had already proved His love by giving His only Son to die on a cross. If He never did another thing for me, that was enough. I didn't know why we had to go through these tragedies, but I vowed to trust God and serve Him in spite of them.

I dried my tears and went to bed. That was around two o'clock in the morning.

At 6:00 A.M., the telephone rang. It was one of the out-of-state adoption agencies where we had applied, saying that they had a three-week-old baby boy waiting for us! Four hours after I had given the matter over to God and quit trying to work it all out myself, our answer came.

Needless to say, I was on the next flight to pick up the baby, too excited to even remember my fear of flying.

The agency worker met me at the airport and handed me the greatest belated Mother's Day gift I could imagine. We named him Russ, after my husband.

Russ was just the beginning of God's blessings. Within the next two years, we adopted another son, Matt, at two days of age. Three and a half months after Matt came into our lives, I gave birth to our third son, Tony Shane.

In just two short years God had filled every bedroom.

⌒ *Martha Bolton*

... *P*ut your trust in the Lord.
(Psalm 4:5b)

Every disappointment or challenge
is an opportunity for growth.

The Miracle of Morgan

To cheat the life of a child seems the worst injustice in the world. When our family saw that one of our own little ones would be challenged, it was devastating to us. We felt knocked to the ground, punished. We were in shock. Morgan was eighteen months old when doctors told us he was autistic. Indeed, he featured symptoms of autism, but the truth revealed that vaccine injuries had caused brain inflammation. His withdrawal from normal childhood included total noncommunication and a myriad of unusual behaviors. Until this time, he was a normally developing child.

We investigated every other cause that might expose him to such symptoms, only to return to the diagnosis of autism each time.

When all our humanly efforts returned no positive-sounding results, I began to realize that only a greater power could sustain us.

I turned to God and prayed as I never had before. Every time I began to pray, my approach seemed lacking. I struggled with my prayers. Then I found the way: The key was to ask God for His direction through our crisis; to promise Him that I would heed His Word, not question it; that I would not analyze His message to me, not hesitate or procrastinate. I fervently vowed to God that if He would let me know what He would have me do to help Morgan, I would act immediately and faithfully, with no reluctance.

Isn't it enough of a miracle to know that God listens and helps us? Of course, it is, but then to realize that His hand is on us and to see results from His counsel is awe-inspiring.

It has been nine years since the trauma of learning about Morgan. He was five years old when he began the process of intensive behavior therapy. As he emerged from his "fog," he was on fire for learning. He is a delightful boy with an ever-present sense of humor, an active imagination, and an outstanding ability to memorize. His drawing skills constantly entertain us, upstaged only by his good manners and sweet disposition.

Never doubt that God listens. What we must do is be sure that we listen. We must listen with our hearts; with our faith. It took God's direction and the efforts of our entire family to get to where we are with Morgan. We were at rock bottom nine years ago when the professionals suggested Morgan would require institutionalizing. We did not give up; we persisted doggedly, knowing that God was directing us. We sought and attained a variety of therapies, taking on each one with the security of knowing that God was leading us.

We have been blessed with Morgan and the miracle of his life. His remarkable recovery is by God's grace. It did not occur to me that as I sought a way to help Morgan, I would help myself. But that is exactly what happened.

— *Karen Brantley*

*O*ut *of my distress I called upon the Lord;*
the Lord answered me and set me in a broad place.
(Psalm 118:5)

IF YOU WOULD HAVE GOD HEAR YOU WHEN YOU PRAY,
YOU MUST HEAR HIM WHEN HE SPEAKS.

Cindy and Sandy

*S*andy and I were twins. From the beginning there were differences. I was older by three minutes. I was also larger and healthier. She was a redhead with brown eyes and I was blonde with blue eyes. Overall, I'd say we got along pretty much like most sisters. We shared a room and fought about things like who would clean which side of the room.

We had very different personalities. While Sandy fussed and worried over grades, I only became concerned when mom and dad did. Although we were quite different, we shared a special closeness. There were periods in our lives when we did "twin-type" things like choosing the same gift for our mother or buying our uncle the same birthday card.

Sandy never had normal problems. Within a four-year period she had emergency gallbladder surgery and a tumor removed from her knee. Then the following year she found a lump in her breast. I remember thinking, "This isn't good, but we'll get through it. It's just one more thing."

Eighteen months after Sandy's original diagnosis, she was diagnosed with cancer that had metastasized on her spine and sternum. This time it hit me really hard. I wondered if we were going to lose her.

Our relationship became especially close. Even though we never discussed it, I think we both knew there was a possibility she might be taken from this world. She did share that despite her constant weakness and struggle, she knew God was there with her. Simple Bible verses about spending eternity with Jesus came alive. She shared that true peace was no longer the absence of trials, but the presence of God. Her biggest concern seemed to be for her family, not for herself.

The following year she was being prepared for a stem cell replacement, a last-ditch effort to kill the residual cancer in her body. She never underwent the procedure for the cancer had spread to her brain.

I emotionally fell apart. For the first time it became very real that within a year, six months, or even the following week, I might lose her. I was devastated. I wasn't ready to let go of my sister.

I believe she knew long before any of us that this was the end. Hospice was called and I arrived back on her doorstep. At one point, she reached out her hand and grasped mine. This tender moment touched my heart. We were not a demonstrative family. This simple gesture spoke more than I can express with words.

I truly believe God allowed her to linger until she had a peace about God taking care of her family. I believe she came to realize that God loved them even more than she did. There were a lot of tears when she died, but Sandy was finally at peace. She would never again feel the pain of her illness.

A man once asked me, "Did you ever feel as if God had abandoned you?"

"No," I told him. "I learned how faithful God is and how much easier hard times can be with Him at my side."

I miss my sister. It's still not easy, but faith lifted Sandy above her circumstances and faith continues to sustain me.

Cindy Schaus

Where, O death, is your victory?
Where, O death, is your sting?
(1 Corinthians 15:55)

I LEARNED HOW FAITHFUL GOD IS
AND HOW MUCH EASIER HARD TIMES CAN BE WITH HIM AT MY SIDE.

A Special Flavor

he end of summer crept up faster than I had anticipated. Louie, my youngest son, was leaving for his freshman year at college to begin studying for the ministry. Why is it you're a little better prepared for the departure of your older children, but when it comes to your "baby," you feel moments of grief that rip at your heart? Could it be that you suddenly realize the season of motherhood, as you have known it, is over? Could it be that this child, who needed to cuddle a little more than the rest, won't anymore? How do you say good-bye to the one with whom you finally got motherhood right?

When each of our children leaves home, there is something missing. It's as if an ingredient is missing in a pot of spaghetti

127

sauce and after tasting it, you wonder what it is that will make it taste like it should. You realize that no one can bring laughter into the house like they can, do little things for you like they did, or share their private thoughts with you as only they could do. Over the years, as each of our five children left, it seemed that the sauce of our home changed according to which ingredients were missing. Sometimes the sauce was filled with lots of flavor, and other times it seemed watered down. Still, you ate it anyway, for you believed that someday it would be better again. But today, with my youngest leaving, I wished the family atmosphere could taste the way it used to, that special flavor, when it had all its proper ingredients.

After leaving Louie at his new school some twelve hours away, I found myself moping around the house and feeling empty. I wondered if he was eating or sleeping right. Was he making friends and did he miss home? I sent up a small prayer asking the Lord to watch over him and make this transition easy for both of us. No sooner had my prayer been said, when Louie called home for the first time.

"Mom, you're not going to believe this. They made me the chaplain of the third floor in our dormitory! As chaplain, my responsibility is to be there for the guys when they need someone to talk with. But guess what else I've been doing on my own each night. After dinner, I visit each room and we have a time of prayer together. Afterward, I give them a big hug 'cause there are so many who are homesick. Now they are all doing great!" With that, he said he had to go. Someone had invited him to play basketball.

"Bye, Mom, I love and miss you."

"Love you too, Louie. Make sure you eat right and get enough sleep. Miss you and I am glad you're doing so well."

As I slowly lowered the phone to its cradle, I quietly asked God if Louie was really okay. God tenderly spoke to my heart.

"Linda, your son is doing fine, and let me tell you why. On Louie's floor there are thirty-six students he gives hugs to each night. With each hug he gives, he receives one in return. You see, one hug is all they need to ease their aching hearts, but Louie needs all thirty-six hugs to fill his heart to overflowing. Now, rest in My peace that surpasses all understanding."

"Heavenly Father, thank You for always answering my prayers. This season of my life needs a new spice, a special flavor. Show me where I am to give, so that my life will once more be full again. In Jesus' name. Amen."

— *Linda Hostelley*

. . . remembering the words of the Lord Jesus, for He Himself said, "It is more blessed to give than to receive."
(Acts 20:35b)

IN OUR GIVING, WE RECEIVE WHAT WE REALLY NEED THE MOST.

My Knights in Shining Armor

*J*im had more than just physical strength. He was my knight in shining armor. Many times each day he would smile and throw me a kiss. He was constantly attentive, often bringing me a sweater or jacket when temperatures dropped.

One winter morning I got up early for a meeting. As I opened the closet to get my coat, Jim came through the kitchen door. Snow clung to his boots and he was wearing his heavy coat over his pajamas. He had shoveled the walk, cleaned the snow off the windshield, and warmed the car for me.

"Oh, good," he said when he saw me. "I was hoping I would get here in time to help you with your coat."

That moment defined Jim. That's just the way he was, always sacrificing himself for the comfort of his family. One night Jim woke me and told me he needed to go to the hospital. Two and a half weeks later, I stood by his hospital bed as he breathed his last breath. A rare cancer had conquered my precious Jim, and he was gone.

Suddenly, when I went to church in the rain, there was no one to let me off at the door. Jim had not only stopped at the door, but got out in the rain and held an umbrella to escort me inside. Now rain brought pain, a reminder that I no longer mattered that much to someone.

Mike came into my life five years later. His quiet mannerisms reminded me of Jim. Mike asked me to marry him. Again, I would be the queen of someone's heart. But I soon learned Mike didn't give of himself in the same way. If he got a snack, it was only for himself. When the family left for church on a cold winter morning, we stepped into deep snow. I often got into a cold car and then waited while Mike left his car door open and went back to the house to tend to something.

It took several years before I took the focus off my needs and put my attention where it belonged—on Mike's needs. He needed to have attention showered on him. Mike needed to be shown the love that I have been shown in the past, for he is my new knight in shining armor.

I have the opportunity to help Mike's armor shine as I polish it with patience, acceptance, and a genuine love. Daily, I tell Mike how I appreciate his touch, his smile. Not every marriage is the same, but ours is going to grow into something very special as we work together on our commitment to each other.

— Linda Dessole Roth

Trust in the Lord with all your heart, and do not rely on your own insight. In all ways acknowledge Him, and He will make straight your paths.
(Proverbs 3:56)

WHEN YOUR IDENTITY COMES FROM BEING A CHILD OF GOD,
YOU BECOME A SECURE PERSON.

Abandoned, But Not by God

As he grew, the boy really never knew any better than to go where he was told. When school would get out in the spring, his mom and dad would always send him off to live with his grandparents in a small town in east Texas. By the time he reached eleven years of age, his grandfather had died and he spent his summers with his grandmother.

The difficult part of the arrangement was the separation from family and friends. Summer is a time when kids should play and relax. The boy was expected to work as a field hand for a man

133

who had been a partner with his grandfather in the farming business. The man came by at 5:00 A.M. each morning and took him out to work on farms all over east Texas. The boy learned to bale hay, cut alfalfa, mend fences, round up cattle, and perform a variety of other tasks.

The boy's heart grieved for his mother, father, and the friends he missed at home. Instead of receiving parental love, affection, affirmation, and involvement, he faced separation, loneliness, and sorrow. Although his grandmother was nice, she was old and tired. The man he worked for, however, was another story.

As the boy grew with each passing year, the man encouraged the boy to utilize his physical and mental talents, skills, and size to accomplish more and more difficult work. In the process the man grew to love the boy and treated him as his own.

God used the man to help bind the wounds of the boy's grieving heart. The man provided guidance, direction, wisdom, laughter, joy, expression, solace, and compassion to an otherwise empty heart.

Once the boy reached eighteen, he went to college and took a direction in life utilizing his brain instead of his brawn. He became a lawyer and practiced in a city hundreds of miles away from his East Texas roots, the farm, and the man.

Although the years passed, the boy never forgot the man. Eventually, the man, approaching ninety, began to suffer from failing health. The boy, now grown up and married with a family of his own, made several trips to visit with the man, his old mentor and friend. In doing so, the boy was able to convey both orally and in writing his love and appreciation for the time the man spent with him teaching and training him. God allowed these two to communicate with words and emotions their deep love for one another. Shortly after these visits, the man died.

God often places people in the lives of others for what may appear to be work-related or mundane activities. Instead, God's plan may be to cause the work relationship to turn into a spiritual growth relationship in which one person is nurtured and matured through the efforts of the other. Sometimes it takes years for the beneficiary of the nurturing to recognize what he or she has received. This is one of the ways in which God provides comfort for a grieving heart.

— Dan Woska

Peace I leave with you, my peace I give to you . . .
(John 14:27a)

YOU'VE BEEN BLESSED, SO BE A BLESSING.

A Life Worth Living

I do not know which I have grieved for more in my life. At five I was sexually abused, at twelve my parents divorced, and at seventeen I awoke to the horrible news that my father had been killed in a car accident. The ringing of our doorbell still haunts me today.

At the age of thirty, I opened a letter and learned that my husband was being unfaithful. As I said, I do not know what I have grieved for more in my life—a loss of innocence, a loss of security, a loss of hope, or a loss of trust. My heart has been shredded, mended, shredded, mended. Now I know this, my heart will always end up mended. With Jesus, the same can, and will, be said about you.

I realized one thing while grieving: Having such loss in my life made it difficult to trust. Why should I trust? So many times it was the loss of trust that crushed me. As I began to read my Bible and grow in the Lord, it was trusting in the Lord that became the core of my healing. Trusting in the Lord enabled me to pull from His peace and joy while leaning on His strength. I cried daily, "Lord, help me to trust You, and please make Yourself real in my life." The Lord answered with a peace that reassured me. He will take care of me, even when the world seems to be crumbling around me. "I will protect your heart," He promises.

He has protected my heart, and He is mending my marriage. Trusting in the Lord has helped rebuild many of the crumbled walls. I now lay my fears at the feet of Jesus. Life is difficult, but I have learned the hard way . . . without Jesus, life becomes impossible.

Grief has many return addresses and seems to be mailed to us all eventually. Even though grief comes in many forms, it continues through us much the same way. Acknowledging your grief and turning toward God will be the start of a life worth living and, most importantly, the life God intended just for you.

Lisa Gilmartin

I came that they may have life, and have it abundantly.
(John 10:10b)

ONE WHO KNEELS TO THE LORD CAN STAND UP TO ANYTHING.

The Blanket

ancer! Mother only had a short time to live. As I sensed our time slipping away, I began to join her in our living room while she worked on a new sewing project—a blanket. I knew from the start how important these times together were for her, and especially for me. There an urgency to my questions. "Tell me about . . ." So with each toiled stitch and brilliant color, I learned about her strength, her courage, and her ability to smile in the face of grim situations . . . even that of her upcoming death.

As each flower sprouted and blossomed on the blanket, she shared stories that shaped her life: the childhood farm in Oklahoma, her wedding, dad's war days, and the birth of each child. I admired her courage and hung on to every word as if it were her last. We chatted about my future. She told me how proud she was that I was going to become a teacher. I tried to make her laugh, and we did laugh until our sides hurt. I made sure that she never saw the tears raining inside of me. All the while, I tucked the stories into my memory.

Although her hands were plagued with pain, she endured the threading of each needle without complaining. When I complained over mundane tasks, she'd say, "Just be glad that you have the ability to do it." These words I have carried into adulthood. Each stitch was tiny and perfect, reminding me of her caring, gentle ways. She'd given so much of herself to others: child care, church work, even in the stitching of this blanket—a labor of perfection to be handed down from mother to daughter. I prayed that I'd glean the lessons she so carefully lay before me: treat others with kindness, serve God wholeheartedly, and live with the highest standards of integrity. I was so grateful to have a living example of such polished character traits. I vowed to continue within me what was so beautiful in her.

Mother died before the blanket was finished. There was just one block left. Shortly after we laid her to rest, my grandmother sewed the last block, a hand-stitched rose. It stands out from the others, not in its own glory, but made different to symbolize me, different, and yet made up of the same things. A reminder that we are still a part of each other.

That was twelve years ago. Every so often, I unfold the delicate work, careful not to stain it with my tears, wrapping myself in its flowers and feeling comforted in the sweet perfume of her memory. Memories made while mother and daughter sat on the couch, sharing their last thoughts. A life coming to an end and a life yet to live.

D. Harrison

Every generous act of giving,
with every perfect gift, is from above.
(James 1:17a)

MEMORY IS A WONDERFUL TREASURE CHEST
FOR THOSE WHO KNOW HOW TO PACK IT.

Safely Home

I am home in heaven, dear ones;
Oh, so happy and so bright!
There is perfect joy and beauty
In the everlasting light.

All the pain and grief is over,
Every restless tossing passed.
I am now at peace forever.
Safely home in heaven at last.

Did you wander so calmly
Trod the valley of the shade?
Oh! but Jesus' love illuminated
Every dark and fearful glade.

141

And He came Himself to meet me
In that way so hard to tread;
And with Jesus' arm to lean on,
Could I have one doubt or dread?

Then you must not grieve so sorely,
For I love you dearly still;
Try to look beyond earth's shadows,
Pray to trust our Father's will.

There is work still waiting for you.
So you must not idly stand;
Do it now, while life remaineth—
You shall rest in Jesus' land.

When that work is all completed,
He will gently call you Home;
Oh, the rapture of that meeting,
Oh, the joy to see you come!

Author anonymous,
Priests of the Sacred Heart

*B*lessed *are the pure in heart, for they will see God.*
(Matthew 5:8)

IF OUR LOVED ONES ARE WITH THE LORD AND HE IS WITHIN US,
THEN THEY CAN'T BE FAR AWAY. (Peter Marshall)

Precious Gift

"Mom," my son Zack said as he stood with his girlfriend on the church basement steps, "Katie is pregnant."

It was ten minutes before our church women's banquet and I was in charge of introducing the guest speaker for the evening. Everything came to a crashing halt as I tried to comprehend what had just been told me. I just stared at the two of them.

We went upstairs where we had a few minutes to talk about the situation in private. An army of different feelings was marching through me. I had always looked forward to being a grandparent . . . but not this way. I felt robbed of the blessing of a grandchild produced in the sanctity of marriage. We talked a few minutes, hugged and cried and they left. I told them no matter what, this child would be loved with all our hearts.

I walked down to the restroom and cried uncontrollably for about ten seconds. It was all the time I had before going out to introduce our guest speaker. I could have won an Academy award that night for the performance I put on, for no one knew what I had just found out. Then I had the very difficult job of going home and telling my husband.

In our children we have such high hopes and expectations. We teach our children to respect God and to follow His moral guidelines. It seemed like I had wasted twenty years of my life. What could we have done or taught differently? I don't know.

I had such a hard time when people would ask about my son and how he was doing. I felt like a failure in having to tell them what was happening in his life. Yet I did not want to take away from the blessing of a little granddaughter. It was a time of such mixed feelings.

When Katie went for her sonogram, she invited me to come along. I saw the child growing in her mother's womb and I wept. I immediately fell head over heels in love with my first granddaughter.

I don't know what the future will bring, but I do know that the good things of the future will quickly erase the heartaches of the past. I will be thankful to God for His graciousness in blessing us with this precious child. For all things work to the good for those who love the Lord.

A lot has happened since I penned those words—it seems like a hundred years ago. Those feelings and hurts are now a distant memory for the Lord has blessed us beyond measure. In January I was present at the birth of my precious baby granddaughter. She is about a year old now and I can't imagine life without her. Today, she laid her cheek against mine, and as I looked at her nestled in my arms my heart ached with love. I'm so proud of my son and daughter-in-law. They are now married and are providing a wonderful home for Mackenzie. But best of all is their renewed relationship with our Lord. For all things do work to the good for those who love the Lord.

If you are facing the same situation we were, take heart, for the best is yet to come.

Bonnie Morgan

Sons are indeed a heritage from the Lord,
the fruit of the womb a reward.
(Psalm 127:3)

BLESSED BE THE NAME OF THE LORD.

A New Chapter

Recently single again, I was forced to give up my country dream home for a small duplex in town. On moving day, my spirits were about as high as the parched brown grass in the neglected front yard. In my former life, "single" was a slice of packaged yellow cheese. Now, it summed up my miserable condition.

Enter Jeanne with the light brown hair and sunshine in her steps. She lifted my weary heart right away. Like me, she had lost the dream of a happy marriage, but didn't flash around her passport to pain. She was on a new journey and invited me to tag along. I signed on for a package tour, an all-inclusive adventure into a wonderful friendship. She got me out power walking, and we shared the same passion for classic movies, good novels, and marathon Scrabble games. With each year that went by, I learned to laugh more and ponder my hurts even less. We did everything together. This single life wasn't looking so bad after all.

Then I met Carl. Oops. I didn't mean to fall in love, but my friendship with Jeanne had opened my wounded heart to trust again. As the months went by, I knew he was the one God intended for me. I prayed, "Please, Lord, bring Mr. Right for her, and we can transition into married life together." Prince Charming never arrived, but Jeanne stayed her upbeat self and relished every detail of my courtship. We planned the wedding, bought the dress, designed the invitations. Yet we never mentioned "splitting up the team." For the first time ever, we were at a loss for words.

The weekend before my wedding, she kidnapped me for a mountain getaway at Lake Tahoe, our last jaunt as single sisters. As we sat in front of a roaring fire, gazing at the snowcapped peaks of the Sierras, the jumbled emotions came gushing out. We felt like Siamese twins about to have separation surgery, uncertain how we would function as we moved in different directions.

My focus would shift to building a strong marriage. Jeanne would form a new circle of friends and activities that wouldn't include me. We blubbered all night about how things would change. No more 4:00 A.M. phone calls, no popping over in her pajamas, no more "what'll we do this Saturday night?"

A chapter was now closing, a new one ready to begin. I never imagined my marriage plans would come attached to an ache like this. How odd that the very part of my past I once scorned could now be one I cherished, all because of a friend. A friend who taught me that if I keep my face to the sunshine, I won't notice the shadows.

After my marriage she gave me time to adjust to my new role, but now we schedule time for just the two of us, a standing Scrabble date each week. I wouldn't miss my "friend fix" for anything.

— Jan Coleman

"This is my commandment, that you love one another as I have loved you."
(John 15:12)

FRIENDS ARE JUST ONE OF THE WAYS
GOD TAKES CARE OF US.

Contributors

Anitha Ainsworth is a member of Christ Community Church, Montgomery, Alabama. She is pursuing her bachelor's degree in Christian Education. Anitha and her husband Richard live on a farm with their animals in Tallassee, Alabama.

Martha Bolton is the author of forty-six books, including *Saying Good-bye When You Don't Want To*, a book for teens dealing with loss. She was a staff writer for Bob Hope for over fifteen years and writes the Cafeteria Lady column for *BRIO* magazine. Martha has received both an Emmy nomination and a Dove nomination, and three Angel awards. She has also written for Phyllis Diller, Ann Jillian, Jeff Allen, Mark Lowry, and Wayne Newton. Martha is married to Russ, a retired LAPD sergeant, and is the mother of three sons.

Karen Brantley, a poet and writer, is originally from southeast Arkansas. Her book *Untold Until Now* (Novascience Publishers), a World War II anthology, was written to commemorate the military service of her father. Karen is interested in art, ancient history, and the pursuit of genealogy, which earned her membership in the United States Daughters of the American Revolution and the United States Daughters of the Confederacy.

Pat Breckenridge lives in Springfield, Missouri, where she teaches a ladies' Bible class. Pat is a busy speaker for Stonecroft Ministries and church conferences, and she enjoys gardening, reading, and traveling.

Valerie Campbell lives in Tulsa, Oklahoma, with her husband Dale and their two sons, Brian and Andrew. Valerie has a B.A. degree in elementary education and has her special education certification. Currently, she enjoys homeschooling her boys and working on family photo albums.

Jan Coleman is the author of *After the Locusts: Restoring Ruined Dreams, Reclaiming Wasted Years*, which weaves Old Testament lessons with powerful stories of ordinary women who found new purpose and fulfillment after loss. Jan is a popular speaker who uses humor to inspire and encourage. Contact her at: jwriter@foothill.net.

Irene Costilow is a wife, mother, and grandmother. She has been married to her "high-school sweetheart" for thirty-five years. Irene is a popular speaker for Christian Women's Clubs, retreats, and other women's events. Her passion for God has led her to be a dedicated teacher of His word.

Cid Davidson says she hasn't done any sky diving, but aside from that she's a former summer stock actress who was converted in a Billy Graham crusade. Cid has been associated with Stonecroft Ministries since 1965 (board of directors for one term, now consultant) and writes for *Progress* magazine, and is currently compiling devotions into a book. She has five children and twenty-three grandchildren.

Chuck Dollarhide is a United Methodist pastor serving God and the church in Minco, Oklahoma. He is happily married to Pat, his wife of thirty-six years, and they have three children and three grandchildren. Chuck practiced as a lawyer for many years prior to becoming a bivocational pastor, and eventually a full-time pastor.

Pam Drummond lives in Fullerton, California, with her husband Bob and their children, Jake, Julie, and Karen. She manages a small insurance agency and writes women's fiction. Pam just recently finished a paranormal suspense novel loosely based on the near-death experience in her story *A Two-Minute Journey*.

Rebecca Marshall Farnbach writes historical fiction, technical nonfiction, and poetry. Her first novel, *Lantern in the Darkness*, a based-on-fact story about Americans in 1840s India, is slated for publication in January 2002—and she is busy writing a sequel. Rebecca is an optician and ophthalmology technician by day, but keeps several writing projects running at all times. She also leads a writers critique group. The most rewarding aspect of writing for her, besides the income, is to hear someone say how a piece inspires them.

Judy Gann is a freelance writer and children's librarian, and she lives in Lakewood, Washington. Desiring to encourage others through her writing, Judy is in the process of writing a devotional book for those who are ill. Her writing credits include prayers published in the book *Crisis Prayers: Real Prayers to Pray in Tough Times.*

Lisa Gilmartin is the proud mother of Macall Montaressa, four, and Elliott Richard, three. Lisa and her husband Brian have been married seven years and look forward to each day together. They are moving to Little Rock, Arkansas, for a new adventure with the Lord.

Teresa Griggs possesses a voice as soft as velvet and virtue as durable as diamonds—she sparkles like a jewel in her Maker's hand. God has chiseled her life through difficult trials. Yet tragedy has not marred Teresa. She has allowed God to shape her heart like a gemstone, polishing each facet to reflect His love, hope, comfort, peace, and purpose. The very joy of Jesus shines from her soul, radiating to all through her compassionate speaking, writing, and singing ministry. This is a woman who has found treasures in darkness, and now shares them gloriously in the light. www.teresagriggs.com

D. Harrison publishes poetry and stories both in the United States and internationally. She is the author of three books and lives in Southern California with her beloved cats Bingo, Kitty, and Mr. Milo. She mostly writes of her passion for nature and its Creator.

Linda Hostelley is the author of *Touched by His Staff*—forty-five short stories on how God cracked open her hardened heart, healed it, and transformed her life to be what it is today. Linda is the founder and president of Mending Hearts Healing Ministries, Millsboro, Delaware. She has had the privilege of ministering at many Christian gatherings, through radio, television, newspapers, in prisons, and on thirty Caribbean Islands. She leads inner healing seminars and also volunteers as a Christian crisis/deliverance lay minister for the upper East Coast. Linda has dedicated her life to "taking in" what others throw away, leading them to the healing throne of Christ and showing them how to reach out to others and become compassionate Christian leaders. (302) 934-9558

Vickie Jenkins is a wife and mother of three and she resides in Oklahoma City, Oklahoma. She is a writer and a medical assistant for an orthopedic surgeon. Vickie's stories have appeared in *God's Abundance for Women; Show and Then Tell: Presenting the Gospel through Daily Encounters; Life Isn't a Game;, Here are the Rules: The Ten Commandments; Taste of Home; The Cherokee Challenger; The Baptist Messenger; Writer's Block; The Writing Parent; The Tribune; Oklahoma Woman;* and she has written over a dozen articles in *The Daily Oklahoman*.

Louise Tucker Jones is an award-winning author and popular speaker. She is the author of the novel *Dance From The Heart* and a coauthor of the Gold Medallion award-winning book *Extraordinary Kids*. Louise has published numerous articles and appeared on several radio and TV programs.

Diana Kruger is an ordained minister and serves as pastor of women's ministries at Renton Assembly of God in Renton, Washington. She holds a master's degree in theological studies and has been published in many periodicals. After losing her son, Diana wrote a book on the subject of loss and how to recover.

Susan Lugli is a Burn Survivor Advocate and the author of "Out of the Fire," published in the *Today's Christian Woman* magazine. She was also honored to be chosen a Woman of Faith, published in the *Woman of Faith New Testament*.

Kathy Collard Miller is the author of forty-four books and a professional speaker. Her latest book is *A Growing Heart: Stories Inspired by the Proverbs*. Check out her website at www.KathyCollardMiller.com (which has a secure shopping cart) on the "Articles" page, "Let's Not Take Our New Life For Granted" and on the "Meeting Planners" page, "Using Visual Aids to Make Your Point More Effective."

Bonnie Morgan lives near West Unity, Ohio, with her husband Mike and two children, Nathan and Bethany. She loves music, reading, and writing and also teaches piano. Bonnie and her family are very active in their church—she praises God for the wonderful family He has given her.

Karen O'Connor is an award-winning author, retreat speaker, and writing mentor. She lives in San Diego, California. You can reach Karen through her website or via e-mail: www.karenoconnor.com or karen@karenoconnor.com

Mike Ozment is married to Debbie and they are the proud parents of two children, Samuel and Mica. He helps his wife run the family business and teaches Crown Financial Ministries classes. Additionally, Mike teaches sixth-grade boys at his church and has coached numerous basketball, baseball, and soccer teams.

Lori Pettus is happily married to the love of her life, Gary. She is devoted to her three children, April, Ryan, and Cody, who are now teenagers. Lori resides with her family in Broken Arrow, Oklahoma, and works as an elementary school counselor.

Carol McAdoo Rehme is a freelance writer, professional story-teller, and speaker, and she fervently believes that everyone has a story to share. Carol feels fortunate to hear so many during her weekly volunteer work in area nursing homes. Her stories can be found in *Chicken Soup* books, including "Expectant Mother's Soul," "Gardener's Soul," "Woman's Soul II," and "Mother's Soul II." She may be reached by e-mail at carol@rehme.com.

Linda Dessole Roth was formerly a Lenawee County Police dispatcher in Adrian, Michigan. Now a freelance writer and CEO of web-based Roth Enterprises, Linda is coauthor with her mother, Dessolee Smith, of the *How to Write a Family Heirloom Cookbook*. Every month she writes a family magazine for her five children, C J, Michelle (and Michelle's husband Brian), Joel, Sandie, and Ronnie.

Carol Sallee is a speaker, author, pastor's wife, and mom of three teenagers. Carol is the founder of To Know Christ Ministries and she can be reached at carolsallee@yahoo.com or on her website at www.carolsallee.com.

Cindy Schaus was born and raised in Northeastern New Mexico on a small ranch. She currently lives in Edmond, Oklahoma, which has been her home since 1980. Cindy is married to her high-school sweetheart, Stephen Schaus. They have two children.

Winn Shields was born in Logan, Utah, February 13, 1946, and raised in Southern California. He is a screenwriter currently living in Texas with his wife and six-year-old son.

Gayle Team-Smith, married to her sweetheart Myles, is the mother of two children, Tifani and Adam. Gayle is an active community volunteer and speaks throughout Oklahoma with Stonecroft Ministries Christian Women's Club.

Denise Springer is a freelance writer and the author of two books on protecting children from abuse: *Confident Parenting in Frightening Times* and *Confident Teaching in Frightening Times.* She lives in Edmond, Oklahoma, with her husband Andy and sons Drew and Tyler.

Joseph Walstad is a graduate of Mid-America Bible College and has worked in the oil and gas industry for more than twenty-five years. His passion for writing poetry was ignited by the urging of his wife Debi several years ago and still provides him much enjoyment.

Jack White is recognized as one of the premier portrait painters in the world. His official portrait of Lyndon B. Johnson hangs in the LBJ Library in Austin, Texas. Jack was named the official artist of Texas in 1976 and his paintings hang in the Smithsonian, as well as other noted museums around the country.

Betty Winslow, a writer and school librarian from Bowling Green, Ohio, loves reading, writing, singing (in and out of church), and spending time with her husband, children, and granddaughter, Kendall Michelle. Her articles have appeared in many publications, among them *Guideposts, FamilyFun, Christian Library Journal, Creative Classroom, Christian Classroom, Writer's Digest,* and *Charity: True Stories of Giving and Receiving.* Betty loves to hear from her readers and can be contacted at freelancer@wcnet.org.

A. Daniel Woska is a practicing attorney in Oklahoma City. He lives in Edmond, Oklahoma, with his wife and two children.

Editors

Margolyn Woods, a former Rose Bowl queen and actress, is a widely acclaimed speaker who has been featured at many national conferences. She has emceed Chosen Women, appeared on the 700 Club, and her personal testimony has been widely read in books and magazines around the country. Margolyn is the author of seven books, including *Grandma's Little Activity Book*, *Ordinary Women . . . Extraordinary Circumstances*, and *God Uses Ordinary Men*, and coauthor with Maureen MacLellan of *Gifts of Kindness, Gifts of Love* and *Words of Encouragement*. She lives in Edmond, Oklahoma, with her husband Roy and their three teenage children, Adam, Matthew, and Taryn. Margolyn's e-mail is Margolyn@cox.net.

Maureen MacLellan is a business consultant for the medical industry in Los Angeles and the coauthor of three other books with Margolyn Woods, *Gifts of Kindness, Gifts of Love,* and *Words of Encouragement.* She is semiretired and enjoys traveling, home decorating, gardening, cooking, and entertaining. Maureen's study of family genealogy includes celebrating the ancient cultures of Scotland and the Highland Games. She lives in Huntington Beach, California, where she cherishes the visits from her adult children, Sherrilynn, Bryan, and Nicolle, especially her granddaughter Tessa. Maureen's e-mail is MaureenMac02@msn.com.